Beyond the Conscious Mind

Unlocking the Secrets of the Self

Beyond the Conscious Mind

Unlocking the Secrets of the Self

THOMAS R. BLAKESLEE

Plenum Press • New York and London

Library of Congress Cataloging-in-Publication Data

On file

LC 96-3314
ISBN 0-306-45262-6

© 1996 Thomas R. Blakeslee
Plenum Press is a Division of Plenum Publishing Corporation
233 Spring Street, New York, N.Y. 10013-1578

10 9 8 7 6 5 4 3 2 1

Printed in the United States of America

Preface

In the fifteen years since I wrote *The Right Brain* (Doubleday, 1980), I have marveled at the practical value of better understanding the physical basis of the mind. Letters from many readers confirmed that their lives were also greatly improved by this understanding. Some even wrote that they had bought copies for each of their friends to share their discovery. Since my own understanding has recently been brought to a new level, I am eager to share my new insights with all who will listen.

Roger Sperry's Nobel Prize-winning split-brain experiments showed us the way to a new understanding of consciousness that recognized that we can have independent thoughts in the right side of our brain that control our behavior yet remain outside of our awareness. These experiments are described in detail in my previous book and also in Appendix One of this book.

Michael Gazzaniga, who worked with Sperry on the first split-brain experiments, continued the work with many additional patients and ultimately concluded that, while the simple right-brain/left-brain model of the mind was an important first step, it was a gross oversimplification. He concluded that there are not two, but actually hundreds of independent, specialized modules of thinking in our brain that all vie for control of behavior in a kind of competitive free-for-all. One of those thinking modules, which he called the "interpreter" module, tries to explain *all* of our behavior, even though it is only in control occasionally.

Carrying Gazzaniga's thinking further, I have come to the conclusion that his interpreter module is actually the physical basis of what we normally call the *self*. In fact, what is commonly called *self-control* is actually behavior under control of this mental module. I have therefore renamed Gazzaniga's interpreter the *self module*. The self module is the specialist in the process called *introspection*, through which we examine our own thoughts. It interprets reality based on certain basic assumptions that are learned in childhood, which I will call the *self-concept*. An important part of our self-concept is the false belief that the self module *is* the mind and can therefore authoritatively explain all behavior. In fact, most behavior is controlled by other modules of the mind to which the self module has no access.

The self module's delusion of power and control is the cause of endless conflicts, misunderstandings, and wasted potential. It is therefore clearly worth some effort to correct your self-concept to one based on how the mind *really* works. To develop this new understanding, I will devote a large part of this book to demonstrating that many of the most "obvious facts" about consciousness are not true. As I will show, our sense of self is a powerful but false illusion—an illusion that is never given up without a fight. A lifetime of habits will not be undone by simply reading a book. Still, I hope to direct you toward a new understanding that you can use to relearn your mental habits. My ultimate goal is to help you find, as I have, that a new understanding of self can help you make sense out of previous enigmas in love, relationships, creativity, sports, and art and help you better understand anger, bad habits, and phobias in yourself and others.

While most psychological theories turn out to be fantasies built on the biases of their authors, I have tried to let sound evolutionary logic lead the way. The principles of neural Darwinism, suggested by Nobel Prize-winner Gerald Edelman, seem to me to provide a solid basis for understanding human consciousness as the inevitable result of evolution.

Acknowledgments

This book is the direct result of my attempts to understand the bizarre interactions of a stormy love affair. From that pain came a new understanding for which I am grateful. Thanks, therefore, to Ms. Ginny Cicciarelli, who started me on the path to discovery by mystifying me with mental illusions.

Many of the concepts in this book are well accepted as part of the *cognitive revolution*, a new collaboration based on evidence from brain-scanning equipment and a healthy dialogue between evolutionary biologists, psychologists, philosophers, and mathematicians. This new consensus, discussed in the many cognitive technical journals, has many practical applications that have not previously been explored. My goal of easy readability and emphasis on useful applications rather than theory is served by confining technical details and references to the Notes chapter at the end of the book.

Credit for many of the concepts in this book must go to the real leaders of the cognitive revolution: The late Roger Sperry certainly deserved his Nobel Prize for starting the whole thing back in the 1960s. His kind comments and support of my previous book will be missed on this one. Thanks also to Daniel Dennett, Michael Gazzaniga, Gerald Edelman, Robert Solomon, and Donald Hebb, whose ideas I have borrowed freely.

Thanks also to my son Robert for the art direction and to the many friends who helped and encouraged me, including Allyn Wiebold, Kyle Culley, Larry Zempel, Mel Walsh, and Carolyn Wesson.

Contents

Beyond the Conscious Mind

Unlocking the Secrets of the Self

CHAPTER ONE

The Self-Organizing Mind

The eyes are not responsible when the mind does the seeing.
——*Publilius Syrus, 1st century* BC

The billions of neurons that constitute the human brain are richly interconnected, not according to a precise wiring plan like a computer, but more like the chaotic tangle of plants in a jungle. In an awesome demonstration of the power of self-organization and evolution, the miracle of human consciousness emerges spontaneously from this tangle of neurons. In recent years a new understanding of this self-organizing process has emerged that revolutionizes our understanding of the very nature of consciousness.

Although our internal mental world feels like an inherent part of our very being, it is really an imagined illusion defined, not by a physical network of neurons, but rather, by a collection of learned concepts that we will refer to here as the *self-concept*. This self-concept is learned in childhood and serves to define the very nature of our consciousness and our sense of self. It provides a mental framework and a model for making sense of the continuous flood of inputs from our sensory organs. These learned concepts of reality are at such a basic level that we feel sure that they are objective and immutable.

Since we learn our self-concept from our parents and our culture, it varies greatly depending on where and when we were born. It profoundly affects our understanding of the world and our ability to function successfully. The very nature of conscious experience in our culture has evolved significantly as the self-concept has evolved.

The *physical* evolution of the human brain proceeds with glacial slowness, requiring tens of thousands of years for any noticeable change, yet our species has repeatedly made giant leaps where major changes in abilities occurred in a single generation. The key to these rapid changes is not in changes to the brain itself but in changes to the *self-concept*.

A similar phenomenon is the reason computer technology has so rapidly taken over the world: Computers can change their abilities dramatically without any change in the physical hardware of the computer by simply loading new software program.[1] Likewise, the abilities of the human brain and the sensation of human consciousness can change dramatically without any physical change: New mental software in the form of learned concepts can transform the abilities of the human brain. When the self-concept changes, the very nature of consciousness and ability to affect the world can also change dramatically.

The incredible burst of progress and creativity of the Greek philosophers and later during the Renaissance in Europe can be attributed to new concepts of self that elevated the power of the individual. When people stopped thinking of themselves as pawns of fate and began seeing themselves as individuals in control of their own fate, tremendous creative powers were unleashed. The concept of the individual self being in control of destiny changed the very experience of consciousness and the effectiveness of human creativity.

Just as a computer can do marvelous new things when a new software program is used, the human potential can likewise change dramatically with revisions in the mental software of our self-concept. Unfortunately, new software often contains unforeseen bugs—undesirable side effects from the very changes that improved performance. The modern concept of a unique and separate self has produced amazing technological and material progress, but it has also left many people with a feeling of emptiness and despair. Several of today's critical social problems, such as increased crime, suicide, and drug addiction, may well be side effects of the same changes in consciousness that brought us material progress.

The stone-age version of self still exists today in the members of many primitive cultures. Their brains, identical to ours, experience a totally different reality. Their world may be under the control of angry or friendly gods. Their experience of time requires no clocks or calendars or frantic efforts to make progress toward a better future. They may in fact have no awareness of their selves as separate entities and no concept of using introspection to look into their own minds. All of these aspects of reality that seem so real and inherent to our consciousness are really illusions constructed in our mind using the self-concepts we have been taught. If we had grown up in a primitive tribe, the stone-age concepts of reality would seem equally real and unquestionable.

If conscious awareness is so relative and determined by concepts we have accidentally grown up with, what difference could it make whether these concepts are true or false? Though we can construct a conscious awareness around any variety of nonsensical beliefs, if these concepts are not in agreement with reality, we will obviously be at a disadvantage. For example, the stone-age culture's experience of reality as under the control of their gods puts them at a distinct disadvantage in dealing with people who have the modern idea of a self that directly controls events.

Our own culture's self-concept has a similarly disabling major flaw. Our concept of consciousness presupposes a mental unity that is a gross distortion of the way our mind actually works. We imagine a unified mental world where all behavior emanates from a singular self. Yet there is significant evidence that your brain is actually organized into *hundreds of independent centers of thought called "modules."* Each module is an independently thinking specialist that evolves to fill a specific need. *What we call the self is actually just one of these many modules.* Though this self module is usually *not* in control, *we are taught to imagine that the self module controls all behavior.* Since this belief forms the very core of our conscious experience, it feels convincingly true.

In this scientific age it may seem amazing that our understanding of the mind could be so basically incorrect that we mistake a collection of separate centers of thought for a singular mind. The reason this is possible is that consciousness itself is nothing but a creative construction of the mind. Our self-concept *defines* our conscious experience so that consciousness will, by definition, confirm our beliefs—no matter how much they conflict with reality. In other places and times many different self-concepts have existed. All have been convincingly confirmed in the conscious experience of the believer. The mind's amazing ability to construct a conscious world that meets our expectations has kept the truth hidden because the illusion is so persuasive.

Roger Sperry's Nobel prize-winning split-brain experiments in the 1960s shook that confidence by clearly demonstrating that when the two halves of the human brain are surgically separated, at least two conscious thinking entities can be demonstrated to simultaneously exist in one head.[2] This discovery led him and others in his team to reconsider the convincing illusion of mental unity we all experience as normal consciousness. The resulting explosion of new multidisciplinary thinking about the mind has been called the cognitive revolution. The falsehood of the single mind concept has finally been exposed and replaced with an understanding of how the mind spontaneously organizes into a collection of specialized modules of thought.

Unfortunately, the mental software of your self-concept cannot simply be changed like a computer program by just loading the new updated version. Your self-concept is so basic that all perception is automatically interpreted in a way that will confirm it—even if it conflicts with reality. To change your self-concept you must ignore what seems to be obvious and carefully examine the external evidence. Old thought patterns will change only gradually, as you learn to reinterpret your conscious experience around the new model, which is based on the actual modular organization of your mind.

In the chapters that follow we will gradually chip away at the certainty you naturally feel about your self-concept. By bringing your self-concept into harmony with the physical reality of your brain's actual organization, many of the mysteries of your own and others' behavior will be clarified.

THE MIRACLE OF SPONTANEOUS ORGANIZATION

Since we are all products of evolution, one of the most powerful tools for understanding the human mind is comprehending how it evolved. Evolutionary principles apply not only during the millennia of our physical evolution but also in the shorter time frame of the development of the infant brain into adulthood. The emergence of a conscious mind from the tangle of neurons in a baby's brain has always seemed like a miracle beyond the understanding of science. A new scientific paradigm is finally providing answers.

The exciting new sciences of chaos theory and complexity[3] are beginning to provide important insights into a whole class of problems once considered too complex for analysis. The 1972 Nobel prize went to Belgium's Ilya Prigogine for his discovery of the basic principles of self-organization. His insights apply to a wide range of problems where simple elements, like the neurons in an infant brain, self-organize to produce marvelous and unexpected *emergent properties* like consciousness.

Self-organizing systems turn out to be all around us, producing complex emergent properties from simple basic elements. These powerful properties emerge spontaneously when simple components act together and are then perfected by evolutionary forces into systems of incredible complexity. The amazing thing about self-organization is that individual elements spontaneously organize without any outside coordinating control.

A simple example of spontaneous organization[4] is a beehive: Bee behavior has evolved so that a hive full of bees has complex properties that naturally emerge without any formal organization. Each bee simply behaves according to its own genetic behavior pattern, yet the hive temperature is regulated, the queen is fed, the hive is defended and repaired, food is stored, and hundreds of other details are accomplished *without any executive in charge of the operation*. Individual bees survive only if the hive survives, *so evolution perfects the emergent properties of the hive*, not the behavior of a bee in isolation.

Bees automatically specialize in certain jobs such as building cells, gathering nectar, guarding the hive, and feeding larvae, *depending on their age*.[5] Experimenters have found that if a certain age group is removed from the hive, that niche will be filled by members of adjacent age groups. Thus, a kind of natural selection occurs wherein an individual bee continues guarding the hive entrance longer if there seems to be a shortage of guards. Younger bees take it upon themselves to graduate to guard duty earlier if a shortage exists.

The emergent properties of the hive are a result of the behavior of the individual bees but are impossible to predict by simply studying the individual bees. For example, though the individual bee is not a warm-blooded animal, the bee colony essentially is. Hive temperature is regulated precisely at an elevated temperature by the concerted action of the individual bees. On hot days some bees will gather water and others will fan the hive with their wings.

THE HUMAN BODY: A COLONY OF CELLS

Each cell of the human body is similarly an internal beehive of activity. Tiny mitochondria independently scurry around, taking care of energy needs inside each cell. Individual red blood cells spend their lifetime traveling around the bloodstream distributing oxygen throughout the body, while antibodies protect it from disease. Again, each individual cell simply does its own thing. The result is exquisitely coordinated activity *without any central control*. The cells, like the bees, have evolved these behaviors because the entire organism was able to survive when the separate cells acted in this way.

Even on a day-to-day level, the evolutionary principle of natural selection is the organizing principle right down to the component cell level. When blood is lost as a result of injury, the low population of red blood cells provides an opportunity for more cells to survive, replenishing the blood. Gaps are filled because they provide opportunities in the competition for survival.

Science used to view our antibodies as reserves to be called up by some mysterious central control, like an army, when infection occurred. We now know that there is no central control. We all have a complete collection of at least one of each of the antibody types we will ever need—like a locksmith's collection of skeleton keys. Each antibody automatically divides whenever it encounters the kind of invading cell it was designed to destroy. By this simple mechanism, the population of antibodies for a particular infection automatically increases dramatically as needed. The large population of that antibody battles the infection and gives us future immunity to prevent reinfection.[6]

The more scientists understand living things, the more they observe this kind of spontaneous organization, which functions with no central control. Evolution encourages cooperative action because survival of the species is improved by it. Our ancestors survived because they evolved antibodies that could destroy disease and had the ability to multiply as required. These antibodies arose at some early point in evolution and filled a gap in the organism's needs in the same way that a plant or animal evolves to fill a niche in an ecological system. "Nature abhors a vacuum" is a basic principle of evolution, so if there is an unfilled niche, something arises to fill it. This principle applies not only to species in an ecosystem, but also to the independent elements in a self-organizing system.

THE EMERGENCE OF MIND

The emergence of a conscious mind from a tangle of billions of neurons in an infant's brain is a miracle not unlike the evolution of intelligent life on this planet. Both result from the same evolutionary principles operating on a vastly different time scale. The spontaneous organization of the neurons in the brain can proceed relatively quickly because it is based on learning mechanisms. The brain's learning capability is based on reinforcement caused by success: Whenever a successful result is obtained, the synaptic connections between neurons that acted to produce that result are reinforced. Chemical changes at the points where the active synapses connect enhance their effectiveness, essentially creating a structure out of the random interconnections.

Spontaneous organization begins when neural connections in an infant brain that accidentally produce a successful result are reinforced. This reinforcement gives them a better chance of producing the same behavior the next time similar conditions occur. The first successful reinforcements are for trivially simple behaviors, but as more complex but related challenges occur, the reinforced patterns may be extended and evolve to support gradually more complex and varied behavior.

Sometimes, a new situation occurs where the previous learning is of no help. In this case *a new cluster* of neurons may succeed and be reinforced. This new cluster will tend to prevail whenever the new situation arises again. This process results in a gradual, spontaneous organization of the neurons into useful specialized clusters, which gradually evolve in complexity each time they are successful in producing a positive result.

We will call these functional clusters of neurons with learning-reinforced synapses *modules* because they can each independently control behavior. The crude first successes of a newly formed module in an infant become the basis for future success in controlling behavior of ever-increasing complexity. The modules compete for control, which goes only to the one that has been the most reinforced in the current situation. This competition between modules produces an evolutionary pressure that continually improves the performance of each module at filling its specific niche. Just as a single-celled animal ultimately evolved into modern man, crude accidental behavioral results of neuron modules can eventually evolve into exquisitely complex behaviors.

Whenever a new challenge arises where the experience of the existing modules is of no help, a new module may be created around a cluster of neurons if they happen to accidentally produce successful behavior. Eventually hundreds of separate, specialized modules spontaneously organize, as needed, to fill the behavioral requirements of the whole person. More often, an existing module's experience helps it to win the competition for control, adding new behavior patterns to its repertoire if it is successful. The module's boundaries grow as the complexity of its behavior evolves. This process whereby randomly connected neurons can evolve into a collection of complex modules of cognition was called neural Darwinism by Gerald Edelman,[7] the Nobel prize-winner who conceived it.

Since each of the modules is an independent center of thought and all function simultaneously (like a parallel computer), more than one module may try to respond to a situation. To prevent conflict, only the strongest module can gain control of the speech or movement mechanisms at any given time (Figure 1). This control-by-the-strongest mechanism prevents us from, for example, trying to say two things at once (although stutterers may be trying to do just that!). We can, however, talk and perform an unrelated movement task, like driving a car, simultaneously.

Note that the "strongest" generally means the one most reinforced by success. The mind thus develops as a collection of individually thinking modules all working in

FIGURE 1. A control mechanism in the brain (represented here by the teacher) selects the *most confident* (not necessarily the most competent) specialized module. Two separate mechanisms of this type decide (1) which module will control speech and (2) which will control body movement.

parallel. Sensory inputs and movement outputs are connected to specific areas in the brain, so modules that require these connections tend to form close to the required connections. Though sensory inputs can be available to all interested modules, the fact that many modules may be simultaneously active makes it necessary that *speech and movement capabilities each be controlled only by one strongest module.* Competitive control mechanisms make certain that only one module controls speech and only one module controls body movement. This competition for control is an important part of the evolutionary pressure that forces the modules to continually strive and improve.

A similar spontaneous organizing process occurs whenever a leaderless group of people gets together—for example, as roommates. Slight differences in abilities gradually intensify as people naturally pitch in to maintain the household. Usually one person, who is neater than the rest, is the first to be annoyed by the mess. That person gradually becomes the cleanup specialist. Another roommate may like to cook and will tend to become the food preparer. With each meal he becomes a better cook and more established as the cook. Another roommate, alarmed by the stack of bills, takes charge of paying the bills and keeping track of expenses. Each time an individual does his specialized task, he become more proficient and more habitual about doing that job again.

The brain undergoes a similar process from birth on, with each thinking module emerging to fill a need—starting with a very basic capability like recognizing the mother's face or grasping her finger. As the baby matures, these simple beginnings gradually evolve into increasingly complex behaviors. Extra groups of uncommitted neurons always compete for control also, but usually they are outdone by an existing, more evolved cluster of neurons already organized into a module with relevant experience.

Occasionally, a novel situation arises where one of the aspiring new clusters of neurons wins the competition because none of the existing modules has any experience appropriate for the task. Whenever a new module gains control, it is reinforced and set on a path to becoming a new specialist. Each success allows the module to become better able to prevail in a similar context in the future. New situations can thus give birth to new modules less frequently as maturity is reached. Usually, an existing module's experience allows it to easily outdo any new competitors. For example, if a module is established for recognizing faces, it will generally prevail when we encounter a new face, but it may or may not win when a child tries to read her first word. Behavior patterns thus evolve continually as conditions change.

An infant's brain development is similar to the evolution of life on a newly created planet. Just as creatures evolved on earth to fill ecological niches, modules of thinking capability develop to fill a person's needs. Again, "nature abhors a vacuum," so neurons organize to meet specific challenges as they spontaneously organize and then evolve to meet the individual's changing needs. Brain modules may also gradually become extinct through disuse if we no longer use them. If we played baseball as a child, that module may become extinct in old age or evolve into a sports module that includes golf. A new module might not form because some of the baseball experience may be relevant the first time we try to play golf.

Sometimes an accident or stroke kills part of the brain. Since brain cells cannot divide, repairs are effected strictly by reorganization using this same evolutionary mechanism. Just as extinction of one species of animal or plant allows another to evolve into its ecological niche, brain damage is healed by the evolution of other modules. They can now succeed where they previously lost to competition with the now-damaged module. Stroke victims must often relearn skills just as a child would, starting from scratch with a new module forming in a healthy cluster of neurons to replace the damaged one.

As early as 1949, Donald Hebb, in the book *The Organization of Behavior*, speculated that neuron structures with synaptic interconnections that strengthen with use would naturally organize themselves into useful cell assemblies. John Holland, working at the then new computer company IBM, began a project to write a computer program that would simulate Hebb's neural networks. The results were fascinating, with uniform arrays of simulated neurons spontaneously organizing into cell assemblies as predicted.[8] In 1980 at the University of Pittsburgh, Steven Smith's poker-playing program based on this same neural network learning-from-success approach easily beat the current conventional program.[9]

Looking at the chaotic nature of the evolutionary process, it is not surprising that each individual's brain develops into a unique organization. The critical decision points where a new module may or may not be formed may be very close competitions whose outcomes could be changed by tiny differences in conditions. Yet each decision starts development down a unique path that may profoundly affect many future decision points. Many reading and learning handicaps are started when learning of the new skill gets off on the wrong track with a strategy that works only in the short term.

Even identical twins don't have identical neural wiring. The neurons grow like blades of grass on a lawn: Though they follow the same rules, the network of roots and blades of grass on each lawn is different in detail. Tiny defects and chance events can eventually develop into large differences. The development of the brain before birth also follows evolutionary principles: Over 70% of the neurons in some specifically mapped parts of the developing brain die in a kind of competition before birth. Even after birth over *1000 neurons die every day,* forcing a continual restructuring. Since neurons cannot divide like other cells, no neurons are created after birth.

Though most of the brain consists of chaotic tangles of connections between neurons, there are some very well defined structures concerned with the connection of sensory inputs and speech and body movement outputs. Specific parts of the body connect to specific places in the brain. The connection point of these mapped structures gives an advantage to specific parts of the brain for certain tasks. The eye, for example, has about 20 specifically mapped connections of preprocessed data to the brain. These maps are specialized for such things as motion, color, and shape. Other mapped connections exist for hearing specific frequencies and for moving or feeling specific parts of the body. Clearly this arrangement causes certain general areas of the brain to be favored to spontaneously organize for certain tasks. Preprocessing structures such as speech recognizing and generating structures can be incorporated in many different modules as needed. Modules can also overlap and use parts of each other's resources as needed.

New brain-scanning techniques such as the PET scan[10] actually monitor the metabolic activity of the brain in three dimensions and in great detail. These scans confirm that most tasks utilize multiple centers of activity in the brain. For a given individual the active areas for a particular task will be consistent (though they may change with strategy changes as the task is practiced). Because of the uniqueness of individual brain organization, the exact physical locations of the modules vary considerably between individuals (see Figure 10, p. 186). This variability is to be expected in any spontaneously organized system.

THE EMERGENCE OF SELF

As soon as a child learns to speak, she begins to be exposed by her parents to their self-concept. At this age the self-concept is a greatly simplified good-girl/bad-girl idea, but it is a start. Her parents may question her about why she behaved in a certain way and about what she was thinking at the time. The module that takes on this task will become increasingly important as it develops into what we will call the *self module*.

Even at this tender age the disassociation between behavior and the attempted explanations by the self module may be obvious. The self module is the specialist in explaining behavior, but in many circumstances the behavior being explained was actually controlled by some other specialist module that won the competition to take control.[11] In fact, there may well be a *fighting-with-your brother* module that actually caused the behavior, but the self module will still try to make the explanations because explaining behavior is one of its specialties.

With practice the self module gets pretty good at making up explanations for behavior. In a later chapter we will discuss research showing that most of these explanations, and the belief system developed to support them, are pure conjecture. As with anything practiced repeatedly, the explanations soon start to have the natural feel of direct, intimate knowledge.

Other cultures view reality totally differently from what seems natural to us. If you had grown up in a culture such as the Chewong tribe of Malaysia, you would naturally explain your questionable behavior as the result of external demons. There are many ways to explain the causes of behavior, but the culturally defined self-concept learned in childhood will always seem most natural to us. A Chewong tribesman would find our explanations for personal behavior ridiculous. In the chapters that follow, we will review scientific evidence indicating that our modern Western way is as misguided as those of the Chewong.

By the time a child reaches the teen years, the self module is almost fully developed. This module is extremely important because it is the specialist in logically planning for the future and also for all calm explanations of behavior. In our culture the self module may assert control of behavior more or less often depending on how the individual has developed. Some people can dedicate themselves to a logical goal and resist all temptations and emotional distractions to achieve that goal. We would say that these people have strong self-control. Others appear to have little self-control and become addicts or criminals. For some people, the self module is seldom in control of behavior except when it comes to making excuses or rationalizing. Good self-control and strong will both indicate a well-developed, confident self module.

CONTEXT SWITCHING

The self-concept most of us have grown up with denies the existence of separate modules and tries to explain behavior as though the self module is always in control. It takes a lot of practice to learn to recognize the different modules kicking in and controlling your own and other peoples' behavior.

The human mind has an uncanny ability to switch modules instantly when the context changes. Multilingual people, for example, can effortlessly switch modules and reply in the correct language when spoken to in either one. Often, different styles of gesturing and reacting to others will also be part of the package. The switch from one module to another is effortless and unconscious: The appropriate module simply wins the competition for control because it feels more confident in the momentary context. Though it is possible that some people could develop the habit of handling a second language in the same module as their primary language, brain damage cases where one language is lost and the other retained provide strong evidence of the existence of separate modules.

A similar instant switching can be observed with other changes in context. Behavior patterns can be noticeably different for each kind of relationship. One person can instantly switch between mother, daughter, boss, and lover—becoming a different person depending on the context within which she finds herself. Teenage boys often develop a unique style for hanging out with their buddies. This includes swearing, spitting, swaggering, and acting disrespectfully. With their mother, however, a completely different behavior module is engaged: a gentle style, often soft-spoken, more articulate, and without profanity. A case in point is the gangster who is a tough, ruthless murderer to his enemies yet warm, loving, and honorable to his family and friends.

Though the current acceptance of mental modules by cognitive scientists started in the 1960s, earlier minds have grasped and discussed the importance of these changes of personality with context. In 1890 William James wrote, " . . . we may practically say that he has as many different social selves as there are distinct groups of persons about whose opinion he cares. He generally shows a different side of himself to each of these different groups." Sigmund Freud grasped the inconsistencies between behavior and the verbal explanations of the ego, which turns out to be quite similar to the self module.

Early in this century Armenian philosopher and spiritual teacher George Gurdjieff[12] wrote:

> Man has no individual I. But there are, instead, hundreds and thousands of separate small I's, very often entirely unknown to one another, never coming into contact, or, on the contrary, hostile to each other, mutually exclusive and incompatible. Each minute, each moment, man is saying or thinking "I." And each time I is different. Just now it was a thought, now it is a desire, now a sensation, now another thought, and so on, endlessly. Man is a plurality.

Our behavior modules have a life of their own: They evolve with time and changing surroundings and may remain inactive for long periods of time. The teenager's hanging out with the buddies module is a descendent of his early childhood play relationships and may undergo significant evolution when he goes to college. When he graduates, this behavior module may remain dormant until a class reunion or may evolve into a bar room or sports context.

Fighting behavior is partly instinctive and partly learned in childhood from observing parents. This specialized fight module can instantly gain control of a person in a context of hostility or threats. Its reaction can be completely inconsistent with the avowed belief system of the self, which may later attempt to explain the action. Often, the memory of events that occurred in a fight may be vague or even incorrect.

Inactive modules have access to sensory inputs, but they may not pay attention to or even understand what is happening when another module is in control. When the self module discusses what happened in a fight, for example, it is like a bystander who observed the fight (which was under control of the fight module) without following everything that happened. When we try to recall what happened in an automobile accident, for example, we may find that the memory is very vague because the self module was busy talking or paying attention to other things before the impact.

Most routine driving is handled by a specialized driving module while you carry on a conversation, listen to the radio, or think about something else. Though you have been making decisions, stopping at traffic lights, and reading street signs, your memory of these actions, as told by your self, is often completely blank when you arrive at your destination.

Many people can hold a conversation on the telephone and simultaneously scan the headlines on a newspaper or write down notes of things to do. Sometimes while we are speaking another part of us has an idea of what to say next or even remembers something totally unrelated. While we listen to the other person in conversation we are often simultaneously planning what we are going to say next. The "cocktail party phenomenon" allows you to be alerted to a subject of great interest being discussed in a remote corner of the room while you are listening to the much louder vocalizations of your own discussion partner.

If a person is angry but speaking words that deny the anger, body language, facial expressions, and even tone of voice often betray the true feelings. In this case one module is controlling speech and another is controlling body movements. All of these examples of parallel thinking clearly demonstrate the independence of our modules. Each is capable of independent thoughts, feelings, and memories—almost like a separate person.

SPORTS AND CREATIVE THINKING MODULES

Sports provide an excellent illustration of the separate modules of the mind. It is not uncommon to talk while playing a sport. There is very little interference because generally the self module does the talking, while a nonverbal module that has evolved for playing that sport simultaneously executes the movements. (Remember, as Figure 1 shows, speech and movement control is resolved independently.) Interestingly, verbal comments on your own game sound like those of a separate person. The self module often becomes angry at bad performance or missed shots and even shouts suggestions. Sometimes the self module will even seize control of the movements—usually with disastrous results. When we initially learn a sport, no skilled module exists to compete with the self. As a result, the self module may win the competition for control, resulting in awkward, verbally directed movements. When a sport is truly mastered and you want to explain it to someone else, you may actually have to watch yourself do the movements, and describe what you see. The self module may not know how to perform a specific movement so it must watch the performance of the module controlling the movement to discover the secret. This splitting of yourself into two separate people is an excellent demonstration of the true independence of the parallel modules of the mind.

Creative thinking is another area where parallel activity of separate modules sometimes becomes obvious. Flashes of insight seem to come from out of the blue, and we have no idea from where they came. In fact, as I write this book, I have no idea where the words and thoughts come from. I have read and contemplated a great deal about the subject, but yesterday I was unable to write a word; today, for some reason, the words flow effortlessly. In its own time some module in my mind starts pouring out the words that I am only too happy to transcribe.

Mozart claimed that entire symphonies came to him in a flash so that he only had to write them down. Everyone has had an "aha!" experience where the solution to a knotty problem suddenly becomes clear. Such moments of insight are the result of mental processes that have been active outside of our conscious awareness while we were doing other things. Clearly, other modules are actively working on problems and doing creative thinking totally outside of the awareness of our self module. The very source of genius may often be a module we have no awareness of except when it occasionally provides us with its gift.

THE MIND AS A COMPUTER

Digital computers, built with circuits a million times faster than the neurons in the brain, are still pathetically dumb in many ways. The reason for this is a basic difference in their organization: The mind has a parallel organization with hundreds of specialized processing modules simultaneously active. Since it is self-organizing, the mind is continuously adapting, modifying, and customizing its structure to deal with the individual's unique environment and challenges. If an additional need arises, a new special-purpose module will spontaneously organize to fill the gap. A never-ending evolutionary process keeps polishing the organization to fit the tasks at hand.

The reason we so often hear the mind being compared to a computer is that our self-concept tends to ignore the other modules that do their work in parallel. The fact is, computers are patterned after *only* the self module and leave out all of the other modules. It is a historical fact that when John Von Neumann invented the computer he was attempting to model his own step-by-step thought processes as seen by introspection.[13] Since the self module specializes in introspection and explaining behavior but can only guess at the activity of other modules, our most important thought processes are usually invisible to introspection.

The self module is language oriented and logical and thinks in a step-by-step manner—just like a computer. Computers, with circuits a million times faster than the neurons in our brain, run circles around us in this type of step-by-step processing. The fact that they turn out to be totally uncreative and inferior to the human mind in so many other ways makes it obvious that they are lacking some very important features.

Since we have plenty of computers to help us in linear tasks, it seems doubly important that we gain a better understanding of those other, less visible, parts of our minds. We must learn to look past the mental illusions created by our faulty self-concept and learn to appreciate and use the other crucial modules of our mind.

Changing our self-concept to accept the existence of other modules is not easy; we have been living with our self-centered view all of our lives. Just as people during the Middle Ages, accustomed to visualizing themselves as the center of the universe, had a hard time accepting the idea of orbiting around the sun, our self-concept will not change easily. It takes time and much effort to change such basic habitual patterns of thinking. The first step we must take is to come to a new understanding of ourselves.

CHAPTER TWO

Getting to Know Your Self Module

*The spirit is the true self, not the physical figure
which can be pointed out by your finger.*
— Cicero, c. 51 BC

Beware of no man more than thyself.
— Thomas Fuller, 1732

Introspection means looking inside your own mind. It is risky business because the act of looking alters the very thoughts you are trying to observe. Introspection is so notoriously unreliable that the behaviorist movement, which dominated psychology between 1915 and 1965, completely rejected it. The cognitive revolution, which is now the dominant force in psychology, takes the more enlightened view—accepting the importance of conscious thought processes but remaining cautious about the accuracy of introspection.

Our new understanding of the mind as a collection of specialized modules of thought neatly explains why introspection is sometimes so unreliable: One module naturally becomes the introspection specialist, so *introspection is accurate only within that module*. All other introspection is imaginative fabrication and therefore unreliable. *We will define the self module as the one that does introspection.* This important module also specializes in many other related tasks that involve calm, logical, verbal analysis and planning. We will call the set of basic assumptions used by the self module to make sense of the world the *self-concept*.

If your self-concept includes a belief that introspection can explain all behavior, then your self module will do its best to fabricate plausible explanations for behavior even when it must depend only on observation and guesswork. The purpose of this chapter is to help you learn to recognize the work of your self module so that your self-concept can be brought into line with reality. With much practice you can learn to make a distinction between real introspection within the self module and inaccurate fabrications.

When you try to use introspection to look into your own mind, you are generally in a calm, logical, verbal state of mind. The mental module that is active in this thoughtful state is what we will call the self module. Notice that in this state you are aware of consciousness and may even be able to follow a verbal train of thought that is a little like talking to yourself.[1] Though you certainly make many decisions without any internal verbalization, when you do think in words and are aware of the process, it is clearly the work of the self module. The self module has no direct access to the thought processes of other modules.

If I ask you your mother's maiden name, it just pops into your mind. If I then ask you to explain how you remembered it, you will draw a blank. Introspection simply doesn't work because the process used for retrieving the name was an unconscious one. If I now ask you how many windows you have in your home, you will probably have to use a logical step-by-step process of visualizing each room and counting the windows. Your self module will be aware of the step-by-step process because the self module is actually controlling the steps of the thinking process. You will probably be conscious of the process and be able to introspect and describe it. Just how you accessed the visual images of the rooms is another matter, because they came from a different module.

If I give you two objects and ask you which is heavier, you will easily indicate the heavier one, but you will again draw a blank when it comes to using introspection to explain how you got your answer. *Consciousness is not necessary for many kinds of thinking, but it does accompany the logical thinking of the self.* The simple reason for this is that the self module is the one that *talks about* consciousness and introspection. "Talks about" in the previous sentence betrays a hidden meaning in our concept of consciousness: It is based on language and our verbal description of the conscious experience. If a person is sleepwalking or in a trance state and we want to see if he is conscious, we probably would talk to him and see if he responds. If he ignores us, we would probably say that he is "unconscious" even though he is walking around and acting otherwise normally.

Language is the very basis of introspection and logical thought; without it there would be no consciousness as we presently know it. Of course there are other kinds of consciousness. People have had the entire speaking hemisphere of their brain surgically removed because of a tumor and yet have retained a kind of nonverbal consciousness and much of their normal behavior and nonverbal personality.[2] Language so dominates our view of consciousness and introspection that these other kinds of consciousness are almost always ignored. It is not surprising that the self module has been able to fool us for so long.

Once you begin trying to look into your own mind to see how common things are done, you soon realize that you are unable to explain most of them. For example, how do you walk? How do you say the word "walk"? How do you climb a ladder? All of these examples are actually quite complex activities that require considerable knowledge for their performance, yet we cannot bring that knowledge to consciousness.

Of course, you can study these activities and develop an ability to describe them in detail, but you would probably do it only by observing yourself in action. In fact, you could probably learn more by observing somebody else. You clearly don't have any direct personal access to this knowledge using introspection. It is unconscious knowledge. The majority of our knowledge and thinking is of this unconscious variety and is therefore usually completely ignored.

Yet, there are certain kinds of conscious thoughts that are easily recalled through introspection: These are the thoughts of the self module. Easily identifiable examples would be situations where you exercise self-control to overcome a natural emotional tendency, laziness, or bad habit: when you don't eat a dessert because it is fattening, or if you have a goal of becoming a concert pianist and you consciously decide to stay home and practice even though you want to go out with friends. These are examples of the self module at work. Free will, long-term planning, and practicing of skills are all the uniquely human work of the self module. It is interesting how perfectly the common usage of the term "self-control" can be taken to mean "under control of the self module." We will use it in that sense.

Though our culture encourages an all-powerful individual self, each person develops a unique self module that may be powerful or weak when it comes to controlling behavior. If you are considered strong-willed and logical, you have a self module accustomed to prevailing even when other modules feel strongly that they should prevail. Mahatma Gandhi and Martin Luther King, Jr., both accomplished great things by overcoming their natural human tendencies to fight against injustice through the usual violent means. Virtually everybody has a fight module that specializes in taking control of violent conflict or threatening situations. These two men had self modules strong enough to prevail even when they were challenged by beatings and massacres. They exercised self-control.

Deceit is another clear area where the self module is in control. If we pretend to like our boss because we know it will help us advance, our self module is consciously overcoming our natural reactions. One of the survival values of consciousness in evolution is that it enabled our ancestors to utilize deception in order to survive captivity by pretending to cooperate with the captor until the opportunity arose for escape. The self module makes long-term plans and can override other modules to accomplish that plan.

Another clearly self-controlled behavior is when we consciously shift direction. Deciding to change jobs, change colleges, get a divorce, or change routes while driving to a new destination are all conscious decisions in which we are aware of the actual thought process.

Logical problem solving, where we break things up into components and make step-by-step decisions, is another clearly conscious behavior. Often, we will use other modules for the substeps of such thinking, but the guidance by logic is a process of the self module. Long-term planning toward any kind of goal usually requires the conscious guidance of the self. Often self-control is what keeps us on track toward the goal, and we are always aware of this process.

If you think for a moment about how much of your actual life is spent doing the kinds of thinking we have just discussed, you will see that for at least 90% and possibly as much as 99% of your day, the self module is *not* in control. If unconscious modules of the mind are usually in control, why do we seem to be continually conscious and able to explain our behavior? The answer, we will show, is related to an amazing ability of the mind to fill in gaps and fabricate a reality that delivers what our self-concept leads us to expect.

THE SELF MODULE AS PRESS SECRETARY

The modern Western concept of the self in control of virtually all behavior puts your self module in the uncomfortable position of having to bluff and fabricate, much like a Presidential press secretary does. Press secretaries have the difficult task of *authoritatively explaining why things were done without actually having any part in the decision process itself*. They do their job, very convincingly, by constructing a model in their mind of the beliefs and goals of the administration based on past statements and acts. This model is used to explain logically all actions of the administration in a positive light. Since consistency is important, interpretations are bent to fit the model, and the model is continually adapted to fit new actions. Many press secretaries have been able to do their job, convincingly, with virtually no contact with the President.

There is strong evidence that most of our introspection and explanations for our actions are similarly done by guesswork. We are brought up with the idea that we can explain all of our actions, and, with practice, we become pretty good at it. As with anything we practice a lot, it soon begins to feel effortless and real. Eventually, we develop a convincing feeling that the self module is actually controlling all behavior—just as we were taught.

Freud and others have taught us that certain bizarre behavior problems are a result of the unconscious mind. Though most people have accepted that idea, we haven't begun to appreciate the extent of normal behavior controlled by unconscious processes. Our mind does such a good job filling in gaps to create the reality we expect that we don't even notice the inconsistencies.

GAP FILLING

A dramatic example of the brain's ability to fill gaps by fabrication is the blind spot in your vision where the optic nerve connects to the retina. This gap in vision is a circle about *ten times larger than the image of a full moon in the sky*. If you close your right eye, the blind spot is about one-third to the left of the center of your vision. Try closing your right eye and looking around the room right now. The brain does such a convincing job of filling in the blind spot

Be sure to keep trying until you see this demonstration work because it is extremely important. We will repeatedly refer back to the ability demonstrated by this figure. The important thing is that your imagination is so convincing in its ability to fill in what is necessary to preserve a nice orderly world that fits your beliefs. This   is a basic part of the way your brain works which shows itself in many other areas also. The filling in   is so convincing that it is hard to believe that   is not real --yet what is filled in is only a   guess and therefore may be dangerously deceptive. This text could as well be any pattern, or a red   spot, or different type sizes. What your brain fills in is what it believes to be there, just as our perception fills in to create a world that confirms our beliefs. If those beliefs are false, as is the belief that there is no hole in this text, we may make serious errors in interpreting reality.

FIGURE 2. Close your right eye and hold the book about 8 inches in front of you while your left eye stares directly at the X. Adjust the book position until the hole in the text disappears. Your brain easily fills in words to cover up for the blind spot in your vision (where your optic nerve enters the retina). This tendency of the brain to imaginatively *fill-in* gaps to make the world seem normal is the cause of much confusion in the world.

by fabricating imagined vision that you may still be skeptical about the existence of a blind spot.

To eliminate that doubt, close your right eye and stare at the X at the right of the block of text in Figure 2. Move the book closer or farther away until the hole in the text disappears. Be sure to hold the book level with the X about 8 inches directly in front of your left eye.[3]

Notice that your brain does much more than simply ignore the blind spot—*it actually seems to fabricate words to fill the gap*! Of course you can't read the words because they are in the part of your vision that is actually fuzzy (though you normally never notice that it is fuzzy), and moving your eye moves the blind spot. This demonstration also works with any pattern or color. If the hole is in a green plaid pattern, the brain will appear to fill in green plaid. If it is in a wallpaper pattern of little pictures of rabbits, it will seem to fill in rabbits. Of course, the brain doesn't really need to *fill in* anything. What it really does is simply not register a change. Our perception is not like a TV camera, but more like imagination, so actual filling in is not necessary.[4]

In fact, your brain fills in much more than the blind spot. The image on the retina of your eye is constantly jiggling around as your eyes move to capture details. Figure 3 shows a trace of the unconscious eye movements of a person simply looking at a picture of a face.[5] (You can see the emphasis on the eyes and mouth.) The eye must constantly move around to see details because *your vision is really sharp only in a tiny area the size of your thumbnail* at arm's length. This area, called the fovea, contains as many sensors as the rest of your retina combined. In spite of this, the mental illusion is of an instantly perceived image that

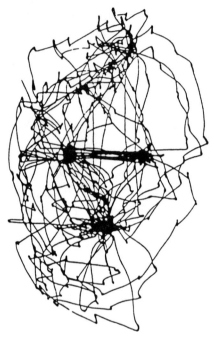

FIGURE 3. A plot of actual eye movements while a person studied a picture of a face. Notice the extra attention to the eyes and mouth. We all make these movements unconsciously to piece together a complete picture in our mind since our sharp vision is confined to a tiny area about the size of a thumbnail at arm's length. We only imagine that we see a nice steady picture which is sharp everywhere. (From *Higher Cortical Functions in Man*, 2nd edition, by A. R. Luria. Copyright © 1979 by Consultants Bureau Enterprises, Inc. and Basic Books, Inc. Reprinted by permission of Basic Books, a division of HarperCollins Publishers Inc.) For additional territory, please contact Consultants Bureau, 227 West 17th St., New York, N.Y. 10011.

seems sharp and in full color over the entire field of vision. Much of the color is also imagined because *your color vision works only in a 30 degree circle at the center of your field of vision.*

Your brain takes this jittery image with a hole in it, sharp only in the middle, and with no peripheral color and uses it to imagine the consistently clear, steady, full-color picture you have come to expect. Obviously, we must be very cautious about accepting anything we perceive at face value because the brain is so good at fabricating to satisfy our expectations.

Most magic tricks depend on the fact that what we see is largely imagined. The magician uses misdirection to distract your detailed vision to something else while he actually performs the trickery in the fuzzy area that you only imagine you see clearly.

BLINDNESS DENIAL

One dramatic demonstration of just how convincing the mind's fabrications can be is called Anton's syndrome or *blindness denial.* Sometimes brain injury leaves the patient totally blind *yet completely unaware of the blindness.* To quote a doctor's description: "Asked to describe the doctor's tie the patient may say that it is a blue tie with red spots when in fact the doctor is wearing no tie at all. When pressed further the patient may volunteer the information that the light in the room seems a little dim."[6]

How could a person be blind and not know it? You should know since, as Figure 2 demonstrated, *you have a blind spot yourself that you don't even notice!* When no visual image presents itself, the brain simply accommodates and fills in with imagination—just as convincingly as you fill in your blind spot. Remember the principle of competition between modules. Without the competition from the visual system, the visual imagination is free to "imagine in" the needed images. In sensory deprivation experiments people usually have strong visual hallucinations. Just think of what happens when you talk repeatedly to someone on the phone whom you have never seen: You gradually develop an imaginary mental picture of that person. This can become shockingly obvious when you finally meet in person. You may be surprised to find that the tall blonde you have been imagining as you talk on the telephone is actually a short brunette!

Imagination is such an important part of color vision that, though you have color sensors only in the middle 30 degrees of your vision, it is difficult to demonstrate this fact to yourself. If you fix your eyes on something straight in front of you while you move a brightly colored object gradually into your field of vision, you should be able to see the color appear only when the object is halfway into your visual field. However, it is important that you don't see the object first or let your eyes move even for a brief glance because once you know the color your brain will naturally fill it in and you will think you see the color. You may have to have a friend help you by hiding the object and watching your eyes against unconscious cheating. If your friend wiggles the object, you will see that it is there before you can recognize the shape. Next, as the object moves in, you will be able to identify vertical versus horizontal, then the shape, color, and, finally, small details. In spite of these limitations, peripheral vision is imagined to be sharp and in full color.

In his early experiments with color, Dr. Edwin Land, the inventor of the Polaroid instant camera, developed a two-color system where images of only the red and the white components of the image were superimposed. The amazing result was a full color image. A photo of a fruit bowl would include purple grapes, yellow bananas, and all of the normal colors. The only problem was that much of the color was *imagined* so that, if they had photographed a fruit bowl where the banana had been dyed blue, you would still have seen a nice yellow banana! When you look through colored sunglasses you can make similar mistakes since they actually block many of the colors you think you are seeing.

Our depth vision also draws on a lot of imagination. If you want to experience three-dimensional television, just hold a pair of sunglasses up to your face such that only one eye has a lens in front of it. When you watch any action scene where the camera is following a moving object such as a runner or sports car, the dark lens will slow your eye's response to motion so that the moving image of the background will lag slightly. This tiny shift in position is enough to give a strong impression of a realistic three-dimensional image. Our brain takes subtle clues and uses imagination to extrapolate them into dramatic three-dimensional vision.

When you read text, your eyes make abrupt movements three to five times a second, pausing briefly on, at most, a few words at a time as you move through the text. Each time your eyes move, your vision goes blank for 1/50th of a second before and 1/30th of a second after the movement. When you read a screen full of text on a computer you are really seeing a blinking series of snap-shots as your eye scans the screen. A fascinating demonstration of this can be made by connecting an optical device for monitoring eye movements to a computer programmed to change words randomly on the screen whenever an eye movement is detected. The resulting display looks rock-solid to the person whose eye movements are being monitored, yet other observers, whose eyes are moving at different times, see a screen amazingly "aquiver with changes."[7]

OTHER FABRICATIONS

The reason for the digression about vision is that it is easy proof of the mind's power to convincingly fabricate, as needed, to meet our expectations. Filling in gaps with imagination is a pervasive characteristic of the mind that is not limited to vision. For example, the auditory equivalent to filling in, called the phoneme restoration effect, allows us to understand speech in the presence of noise from a jetliner or a bad telephone connection. Gaps in the sound are unconsciously filled in by the brain. Another example is the "proofreader effect," which causes us to not see obviously missing words and spelling errors when we read a manuscript.

More to the point is the equally powerful illusion the mind produces to satisfy the expectations of our self-concept. We expect to be able to explain all of our behavior by using introspection, so the self module obliges by filling in using imagination. Just as part of what we see visually is real and part is imagined, part of introspection is real and part is fabrication. The big difference is that, while visual filling in is almost always harmless, if we take our fabricated introspection seriously it can seriously impede our understanding of our own actions and our interaction with others. We all have personal beliefs and desires that our self module can discuss. We sometimes act on those beliefs when the self module is in control, but most of our behavior is actually controlled by other modules. Most of the time the self module is *not* in control.

There is a large body of experimental literature on cognitive dissonance that demonstrates that beliefs are often constructed to harmonize with our actions, rather than vice versa. Cognitive dissonance is created when our behavior doesn't match our actions, and numerous experiments show that people often eliminate that dissonance by changing their avowed beliefs after such a conflict. In one such study,[8] students were first given a questionnaire to assess their beliefs about cheating on tests. Some of the students strongly disapproved of cheating, while others thought it not so bad. The students were later given an important exam structured so that it was easy to cheat; the subjects didn't know it but the experimenters were carefully monitoring them for cheating. Some of the students who had said they strongly disapproved of cheating did cheat on the test, while some of the others, who didn't disapprove strongly, were nonetheless honest on the test.

After the test, the students were again questioned about the morality of cheating. The students whose behavior had been in conflict with their previously stated beliefs were found to have *changed their beliefs to match their behavior*: If they had cheated, they now felt that cheating was not so bad; if they had been tolerant of cheating before, but been honest on the test, they were now more disapproving of cheating.

It appears that, in some cases, the decision to cheat was made by a module other than the self, but the self, as press secretary, modified the belief system so it would no longer conflict with its own observed behavior. Of course, a strong-willed student could have consciously exercised self-control to override the temptation to cheat. However, as the results showed, this often doesn't happen.

WHY DID YOU DO THAT?

When we practice something enough to become an expert, we often get the feeling of a kind of sixth sense or feel for the subject. For example, chess masters say they can feel that a piece on the chessboard is in danger before they figure out the cause of the danger. After a lifetime of explaining reasons for our behavior, the self module gets just such a feeling. Psychologists have performed numerous experiments that indicate this confidence may be mistaken. For example, one group of experimenters[9] set up a mock consumer survey in a commercial establishment. They placed four identical pairs of nylon stockings on display and then asked passersby to evaluate them and pick the one they felt was of the best quality. They were surprised to find a large 4:1 bias for choosing the stockings displayed farthest to the right. (This is probably because English-speaking people habitually scan left to right so the right side was the last examined.) When the subjects were asked why they chose the stockings they did, *nobody* mentioned the position in the array, even though that was usually the real, though unconscious, reason for their choice. When the examiner suggested that it could be related to display placement, virtually all subjects denied it, "usually with a worried glance at the interviewer suggesting that they felt either that they had misunderstood the question or were dealing with a madman."

In another study, 81 subjects were asked to memorize a list of word pairs. Some of the word pairs were included to see if they would affect the results of a later, different word association task. For example, when subjects memorized the combination "ocean–moon," it might make them more likely to think of "Tide" when they were later asked to name a detergent. When the results were tabulated, the semantic cuing was found to double the frequency of target responses. Subjects were asked in an open-ended way why they had given their responses, and, though they could still remember the word pairs, they almost never mentioned the word pair as a reason for giving a particular response. Instead, they gave answers like "Tide is the best-known detergent," or "My mother uses Tide," "I like the Tide box." When the experimenter suggested that the word pairs could have influenced the choice, only about one-third of the subjects would admit that the words probably had an effect.

During other, similar experiments, researchers also quizzed people who *didn't* participate in the experiment about what they thought people would do in the situation presented by the experiment. They found an excellent correlation between what an average outsider would *theorize* about behavior in that situation and what the experimental subjects said about what actually caused their own behavior. In other words, *your insight about your own behavior may be no better than the theorizing of another person.* The self module seems to have no private knowledge of the reasons for behavior not under its control.

"I WASN'T MYSELF"

"I wasn't myself" is a common phrase people use to excuse bad behavior. It shows a self-concept that agrees with the one we are presenting here. However, it also shows a dangerous denial of responsibility for personal behavior. Society recognizes a difference between self-directed behavior and the instinctive reaction of other modules by making a legal distinction between murder and manslaughter. First-degree murder is clearly behavior directed by the self, involving long-term planning. Manslaughter, on the other hand, is probably the work of the fight module.

Your personality is an emergent property of the collection of specialized modules of thought that have formed in your brain. They are all part of you, and as a person, you will be held responsible for all of their actions. President Truman's attitude, "The buck stops here," is a healthy one to adopt when explaining your own behavior. The President doesn't control everything directly either, but must depend on specialists to do most of the actual work. A commitment to take responsibility, rather than pointing the finger of blame, is a healthy one. A strong self module is capable of exercising self-control when it sees bad behavior. As with being President, the key to success is *not* invariably in taking personal control of everything but in nurturing and supporting the specialists while accepting responsibility for the results. An effective person is similar to a small company with skilled and relatively autonomous specialists doing most of the work and a nurturing president (the self) acting as spokesperson, personally doing only things the specialists cannot do. Occasionally, however, situations may arise where the president (or self) must momentarily seize control to prevent disaster.

Whether we like it or not, we will be held responsible for the actions of all of our modules. Prisons are full of people who weren't themselves at the time of the crime. Good advertising and salesmanship is seldom directed at your rational self module. Unfortunately, it is the self module that must make good on the checks written by the less rational parts of your mind.

CHAPTER THREE

Time and Consciousness

*Illusions commend themselves to us because
they save us pain and allow us to enjoy pleasure instead.
We must therefore accept it without complaint when
they sometimes collide with a bit of reality
against which they are dashed to pieces.*
—— *Sigmund Freud*

When we hear a church bell ring and look at the steeple, we feel a very real consciousness of its being there—across the street. Yet the mental picture we have is really almost pure imagination: The vibration of our eardrums inside our head is interpreted, not as something happening inside our head, but rather as a sound across the street. The upside-down image on our retina, also inside our head, is turned into a vision of a church across the street. Clearly, these sensations are imaginative, mental constructions rather than a simple factual awareness of what is happening to our sensory organs.

Consciousness is marvelously creative and deceptive, constructing an orderly picture of the world imagined into a format that will be most useful for survival. Our perception of time undergoes a similar creative distortion to help us make sense of things. For example, when we watch a movie, we are really seeing a series of still pictures: If a person in a movie is raising his hand, we may actually see one frame with the hand at waist level and the next with

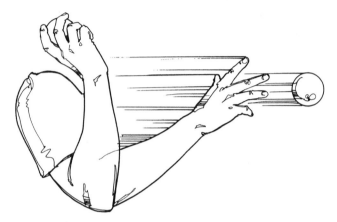

FIGURE 4. When we watch a movie of something in motion we only imagine that we see continuous movement. A movie of someone throwing a ball may only actually show the arm in two positions, yet we imagine that we see an arm in smooth motion. Our perception must be delayed in time because otherwise, at the instant when the arm was halfway extended, we wouldn't even know that it was moving since we wouldn't yet have seen the next frame.

the hand at shoulder level. What we experience is a smooth movement of the hand traversing all of the intermediate positions. When the hand appears to be halfway up *we must have already seen the next frame* or we wouldn't know that the hand was moving up. Clearly, our sense of time must be distorted or delayed in consciousness to make this possible (Figure 4).

Another simple demonstration of our creative interpretation of time is called the phi phenomenon. When two light bulbs, reasonably close to each other, are alternately blinked, we will see them as a single light moving smoothly back and forth. If the two lights are different colors we will see a light moving back and forth and *changing color in the middle.* How can we know what color the light should be in the middle unless we have already seen the next color? Our sense of time must obviously be distorted to make this possible. A built-in delay in perception would do the job but would be a disaster in the many situations where fast response is a matter of life and death. Evolution would simply not allow it.

The real explanation is that our mind is able to *revise the memory of what we saw, after the fact,* to incorporate information that arrives later without our noticing it. As an example, read the following sentence aloud to someone: "Rapid righting with his uninjured hand saved from loss the contents of the canoe." Halfway through the sentence the second word will seem to be "writing," yet the second half of the sentence clarifies the meaning to "righting." When the sentence is finally correctly understood, the original wrong meaning is forgotten by most people as their memory revises itself to remove the confusion.[1] Revision after the fact to make things make sense is a normal characteristic of memory.

The mind uses considerable creativity in constructing a reality for us that makes sense. The process of filling in a sense of smooth movement from the series of still pictures on the movie screen is simply another variation of the filling in that we saw with our visual blind spot in Figure 2. It seems that filling in and fabricating to tidy up reality is a basic characteristic of consciousness.

BACK-DATED MEMORY

If you are driving a car and talking simultaneously and a child darts into the road, you will immediately slam on the brakes to avoid hitting him. Your consciousness of the braking and your emotions will actually come after the braking has already occurred. Your passenger may even hear you finish saying a word while your foot is hitting the brake, but your memory will make it seem like you consciously hit the brake. Though the braking was actually done by another unconscious module of the brain or spinal reflex, your memory is backdated to keep things tidy and maintain the illusion of conscious control (Figure 5).

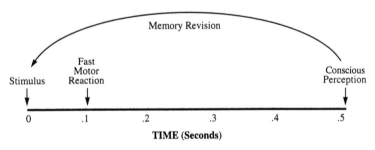

FIGURE 5. Backdating of consciousness. When asked to press a button in response to a touch to the skin, subjects are able to react in only 1/10th of a second. Other tests show that it takes 1/2 second before the subject is conscious of the touch. In spite of this, the button pressing seems like it was done consciously. We appear to routinely revise our memory of the timing of an event to maintain our belief in conscious control.

Benjamin Libet, of the University of California in San Francisco, experimentally demonstrated that consciousness of touch sensations may in reality be delayed more than we remember. He used brain surgery patients with wires connected directly to a part of the brain that receives touch sensations. Electrically stimulating this area can block the sensation of touch.[2] The amazing thing is that the sensation is still blocked even when the electrical stimulus starts 0.2 second *after* a touch! Since it only takes 0.1 second to respond physically to a touch (for example, pressing a button), it is clear that consciousness is not involved in the response. To make everything look tidy, our consciousness simply revises its memory of when the touch sensation was felt—a little like fudging the books, or backdating a contract.

Another fascinating experiment by British neurosurgeon W. Grey Walter[3] used electrodes implanted at the point in the motor cortex of the brain associated with index finger movement. He amplified the electrical signal at this point and connected it to the advance mechanism on a carousel slide projector. He gave the patients the slide-advance button and told them to push it whenever they wanted to see a new slide. This was a free decision based on boredom or curiosity about the next slide. What he didn't tell them was that the button wasn't even connected. The patients were amazed to see the slides advancing just as they were "about to" press the button but before they had actually made their decision to press. Their free and conscious decision to look at the next slide produced an electrical signal in their brain *before* they actually decided to press the button! It appears that many of the decisions that we think are conscious actually originate somewhere else in the brain. Our memory is tidied up to place the conscious decision before the action.

Libet did another experiment[4] with the timing of consciousness that didn't require an internal connection to the brain. He attached electrodes to the scalp of the subjects to electrically detect the "readiness potential" that occurs before we make voluntary movements. He asked the subjects to flex their wrist at random times and to take note of the position of a spot on a rotating clock disk at the instant they consciously decided to do the flexing. He found that he could detect the readiness signal about a third of a second *before* the time subjects became aware of their conscious decision.[5] Again, the actual decision to flex must have come from another module—before consciousness of the decision. To maintain our feeling of consistency and self-control we simply adjust our memory to keep things tidy. While this sounds dishonest, it is really not that different from filling in our visual blind spot with phony words.

IS CONSCIOUSNESS IN CONTROL?

All three of these experiments show that our feeling of conscious control may often be just another illusion created by the self module. The actual impulse to press the button to see another slide, for example, comes from another mental module. The self module later becomes aware of the action and backdates memory to maintain the illusion of self-control. Consciousness seems to fabricate a narrative of our actions that fits our self-concept as controller of all actions. When we use introspection we are asking our self module for a narrative of what happened. It should not be surprising that this self-centered point of view could be a distortion of what actually happened—especially when you consider that the self module is not even aware of the existence of other modules of thinking or of the parallel nature of the mind.

One of the clearest demonstrations of this delusion of the self is a phenomenon called "blindsight," which is the opposite of blindness denial. A stroke or brain injury can completely destroy all awareness of vision, usually on one side or the other. Though the patient insists he sees nothing, careful testing will show that he can do much better than chance at "guessing" about shapes or flashes of light presented in the blind area. It appears that connections are still intact to other, unconscious, modules that deal with reacting to vision. The fact that the patients refer to their responses as "guessing" or a "gut feeling" is yet another demonstration of how the self module maintains the fiction that it controls everything.[6] Hunches and intuitive judgments are probably the result of similar weak communications between other modules and the self module.

Another similar demonstration of modularity is seen when a stroke destroys a person's ability to recognize faces of friends and family. If skin conductance is monitored (as in a lie detector) while the patient views photographs of strangers and friends, skin conductance sometimes clearly shows that recognition has occurred at an unconscious level.[7] Clearly the self module is not aware of much of what goes on in our brain.

One of the basic principles of evolution is that nothing can ever be totally reorganized or redesigned. Changes must always occur by mutations that gradually add to or modify existing structures and yet maintain functionality. Since consciousness is something added late in evolution, it must have been added on top of existing brain capabilities. It can add new abilities and possibly override older behaviors, but the basic behavior found in lower animals continues to function as it always has. Even the visible structure of the brain shows the layers resulting from evolution: Deep inside our brain is the reptilian brain, an evolutionary remnant of our reptile ancestry that still performs many basic functions. This is covered by a newer mammalian brain, which in turn is enveloped by the newest part of our brain, the cortex. Though many other animals have a cortex, it is the massively evolved cortex that gives us our edge over other animals.

The verbal, logical self module is very much a product of language; it is, in a sense, constructed out of language. Though most of our behavior continues to be produced by the old preconscious structures, our self module imagines our behavior as something that it alone initiates, because that is our learned model of reality. With such a distorted picture of reality, it is not surprising that we have such problems understanding each other. The first step in getting along with others must be understanding ourselves. The self module may have veto power on behavior and it may even direct certain logical actions, but the vast majority of behavior is controlled by other modules and lower parts of the brain unseen by the self.

Though the illusion of control is strong, evolutionary logic, and experiments like the ones just discussed, tell us that consciousness is more often simply an observer of behavior. Even something as simple as a decision to look at the next slide in a slide show actually comes from an unconscious part of the brain. Consciousness of the decision comes later, accompanied by a strong conviction that consciousness made that decision.

IS CONSCIOUSNESS CONTINUOUS?

If consciousness and introspection are so unreliable, how can we survive at all? Luckily, 99% of the time most people don't use either of them. When you are thinking and reading about consciousness it is particularly easy to overestimate its presence. The fact is, *anytime you ask yourself, "Am I conscious now?" the answer will always be yes! Since introspection is done by the self module, whenever you use introspection you will see the self module in control.* This is a little like the Heisenberg uncertainty principle in physics: The act of observation changes what we are trying to observe. To really understand how our minds work, we must use experiments and external observations and ignore the strong conflicting impressions produced by introspection.

The powerful illusion that we are always conscious is a hard one to ignore. We always see consciousness when we look for it, so it seems obvious. The simple fact is that the act of asking ourselves whether we are now conscious implies a conscious train of thought. When we are not conscious, which is often, we cannot notice it because that would require consciousness. To take a similar example, if you could ask a flashlight in a dark room if there were any dark corners, it would answer, "no." Since there is light wherever the flashlight turns, it would never see any dark places.[8]

On the other hand, if you try hard to quiet your mind and think about nothing you will find that there is always something—a noise, a breeze, a memory image, or a random thought. The problem is, the effort not to think always engages your self module. Willpower is the domain of the self, so the harder you try not to think, the less chance you have of succeeding. There is a way to quiet the self module, but it does not involve willpower: If you do any task that firmly engages another module of thought, the self module will instantly fall silent.

Skill activities that require concentration, such as art, music, sports, dancing, or nonroutine work, can put you in a *flow state* where the self module is quiet and time seems to stand still. When you have been in a flow state for an extended period of time and your self module reasserts itself, you may feel that there is a time gap in your memory where you don't even know what happened. You may look at the clock and remark about how time flies. The activities that will make this happen always require skills in which the self module is not proficient. This guarantees that the self module will lose the competition for control. While the gap in consciousness is noticeable after such extended periods, normal day-to-day existence contains occasional brief bursts of self-consciousness.

Since the self module is often nagging us with what we should do, it can feel quite refreshing to have this nagging silenced for extended periods. Drinking alcohol and smoking marijuana both weaken the hold of the self module and silence the nagging. Alcoholics are often people who are nagged by a feeling of not doing what they should be doing. When they are drunk they tend to live in the moment and not worry about the long-term planning of the self. The gap in memory experienced by some alcoholics indicates that their self module has been disabled while they were drunk.

One reason people develop hobbies is that they can quiet the nagging self module by putting themselves in a pleasant flow state for extended periods of time. The quieting of the self module and living in a continual flow state are common goals in Eastern religions. Meditation is a regular exercise directed at quieting the self. It could be very useful for Westerners, but it is often made very difficult by our strong habit of using self-control to accomplish things. When we try to use willpower, it engages the self module, which defeats the whole purpose of meditation. Learning to accomplish things by letting go takes a lot of practice, but the payoff is considerable.

CHAPTER FOUR

Memory Illusions

Nothing is easier than self-deceit.
For what each man wishes, that he also believes to be true.
——Demosthenes, 320 BC

Gaps in memory are filled in by consciousness just as convincingly as the blind spot's gap in our vision. While visual filling in seldom causes any trouble, false memories are the cause of countless arguments and misunderstandings. The problem is that fabricated memories feel so completely and convincingly real.

The bizarre blindness denial we discussed earlier has an exact equivalent in memory loss. When people abruptly lose their memory as a result of stroke or injury, more than half of them don't even notice their amnesia: They simply, and naturally, begin making up stories to replace their missing memories. They are totally unaware that the stories are false and will volunteer endless details, thinking that they are real memories.

One study of 101 serious brain injury patients at Walter Reed hospital found that 60% made up stories (confabulated) to replace actual memories of their injury and other aspects of their life as soon as they regained consciousness.[1] It seems that when the normal source of information is missing, it is quite common for consciousness to fill in with fantasy. Just as the blindness denial patients imagined vision when their real vision was destroyed, people who lose their memory often fill in the gap with imagination. In both cases the patient doesn't even notice the difference. Even in normal memory recall, missing details are often filled in. When the memory is totally missing, the filling in becomes *confabulation*: a completely fabricated story believed by the teller.

The reason confabulation is so common after brain damage is simply that it is a habitual part of normal behavior. Just as we all unconsciously fill in the blind spot in our vision, we often fill in gaps in memory without even knowing it. When we recall a memory, we feel certain we are really remembering every detail, yet it is easy to prove otherwise. For example, visualize a penny in your mind's eye. Now, try to draw it in detail—including all of the words and numbers in their correct location. If you were able to do it correctly you are one in a hundred. The fact is that our mental images *seem* to be detailed but actually prove otherwise when we try to get specific.

If you close your eyes and try to visualize your hand you should be able to tell which finger is the second longest by just looking at the mental image. The fact is you probably can't because you have never noticed that detail. Yet, the image feels convincingly complete till you push it for details. We seem to be able to ignore missing details and feel that they are filled in even when they are not. The words that seemed to fill in your blind spot in Figure 2 are similar. They seem normal, yet we can't read them.

Recall a recent memory, such as entering the room in which you now sit and picking up this book. Visually, remember what it was like. You may see an image of yourself walking into the room, sitting down, and opening up the book. If you see a memory image like that, you know it is pure imagination because your eyes never saw anything like that. In reality, what you saw was more like moving views of the room—as though your eyes were a TV camera. You may have seen your hands holding the book and possibly your knees but, unless you were watching yourself in a mirror, you didn't see yourself at all. An imagined image that seems logical can feel convincingly like a real memory.

MEMORY GAP-FILLING

When we consciously recall a memory, we creatively reconstruct it—sometimes from tiny fragments that are actually in our memory. What we tend to construct is what should have been, rather than what actually occurred. If we misunderstand what somebody says, the memory will be of what we *thought* we heard, not what we actually heard. If we misunderstand what we see, the memory will be of what we *thought* we saw, rather than what we actually saw. Memory is not a recorder of raw sensations, but rather a very concentrated and filtered record of what we understood, sometimes modified into what we now think it should have been.

Sometimes a hypnotist can seem to bring out more details from memory, but when those details are checked they often turn out to be fabrications. The subject tries to satisfy the hypnotist's request, even if it means making up details. This is easy to do because we do it all the time in the normal filling-in process of consciousness. Subjects will even tell details of their lives in the future or in previous lives if asked to under hypnosis. Experiments have shown that hypnotism is no better at aiding recall of details than carefully taking some time to recall the details in a normal state.

Many people consider themselves quite good at retelling complete conversations in minute detail. If the conversation has been tape recorded, we have a unique opportunity to check the accuracy of the recall. One classic example of such recall is a matter of public record from the infamous Watergate scandal of 1972. John Dean, President Nixon's assistant in charge of containing the scandal, submitted a 245-page statement to the investigating committee recounting events and conversations during the cover-up. Soon after his testimony, it was revealed that Nixon had tape recorded all of the conversations. Comparing the recall to the actual conversation provides a fascinating picture of memory filling in and creative modification at work. Here is an excerpt from Dean's account of his meeting with President Nixon the day after the grand jury indicted the five Watergate burglars along with Hunt and Liddy, thus excluding the White House from blame:

> The president asked me to sit down. Both men appeared to be in very good spirits and my reception was very warm and cordial. The President told me that Bob—referring to Haldeman—had kept him posted on my handling of the Watergate case. The President told me I had done a good job and he appreciated how difficult a task it had been and the President was pleased that the case had stopped with Liddy. I responded that I could not take credit because others had done much more difficult things

than I had done . . . I told him that all I had been able to do was to contain the case and assist in keeping it out of the White House. I also told him there was a long way to go before this matter would end and that I certainly could make no assurances that the day would not come when this matter would start to unravel.

When the actual White House tapes of the conversation are compared to Dean's recall, we can see the creativity of memory recall. To quote Neisser's article[2] in a medical journal:

Comparison with the transcript shows that hardly a word of Dean's account is true. Nixon did not say any of the things attributed to him here: He didn't ask Dean to sit down, he didn't say Haldeman had kept him posted, he didn't say Dean had done a good job (at least not in that part of the conversation), he didn't say anything about Liddy or the indictments. Nor had Dean himself said the things he later describes himself as saying: that he couldn't take credit, that the matter might unravel someday, etc. (Indeed, he said just the opposite later on: "Nothing is going to come crashing down.") His account is plausible, but entirely incorrect.

It is apparent that Dean recalled very little of what was actually said. Yet he was confident enough of his reconstruction of the conversation to repeat essentially the same account in sworn verbal testimony. What he recalled was not what was actually said but a fantasy of what *should have been said* from his personal point of view. Again quoting Neisser's article:

In Dean's mind Nixon *should* have been glad that the indictments stopped with Liddy, Haldeman *should* have told Nixon what a great job Dean was doing: most of all, praising him *should* have been the first order of business. In addition Dean *should* have told Nixon that the cover-up might unravel, as it eventually did, instead of telling him it was a great success (as Dean actually did).

When memories are filled in there is a strong tendency to unconsciously use wishful thinking and to distort the memory in a self-serving way. The problem is that we may be totally unaware that we are fabricating. The filling-in process is so natural and convincing that we may honestly swear that we are remembering clearly. Once a memory has been retold falsely, a new and stronger memory of the retelling is created. Each time the story is recalled we become more certain that it really happened. Many courtroom battles end up with conflicting eyewitness testimony: Two people, having experienced the same conversation, each unconsciously fills in in a way that enhances his own self-image. With neither consciously lying, we end up with two people swearing, under oath, to conflicting versions of the same conversation.

Even with written contracts, a battle still often results since each side swears that he remembers a different interpretation as the true intent of the contract. Usually both sides honestly believe their own interpretation, which is always one that favors their side. Each time a fabricated or distorted memory is discussed with friends or lawyers it is reinforced so that the person becomes even more certain of its truthfulness.

CHANGING MEMORIES

Stories of cute things you did as a child that are repeatedly retold at family gatherings soon take on the feel of actual memories. Sometimes the stories gradually change over time and may end up only loosely related to what really happened. You can easily bring back images of yourself acting out the current version, which has the convincing feel of genuine memories.

Jean Piaget, the famous child psychologist, tells a personal story in his *Plays, Dreams, and Imitation of Childhood*[3] that illustrates this beautifully:

> . . . one of my first memories would date, if it were true, from my second year. I can still see, most clearly, the following scene, in which I believed until I was about fifteen. I was sitting in my pram, which my nurse was pushing in the Champs Elysees, when a man tried to kidnap me. I was held in by a strap fastened around me while my nurse bravely tried to stand between me and the thief. She received various scratches, and I can still see vaguely those on her face. Then a crowd gathered, a policeman with a short cloak and a white baton came up, and the man took to his heels. I can still see the whole scene, and can even place it near the tube station. When I was about fifteen, my parents received a letter from my former nurse saying that she had been converted by the Salvation Army. She wanted to confess her past faults, and in particular to return the watch she had been given as a reward on this occasion. She had made up the whole story, faking the scratches. I therefore, must have heard as a child, the account of

this story, which my parents believed, and projected
into the past in the form of visual memory.

Memory is a dynamic thing that not only fades but
grows and changes with time. As the Piaget story shows,
memories can even be created after they are supposed to
have occurred. Memories are reinvented whenever we
recall them and are changed in the light of later experiences. "I don't know what I ever saw in . . . " is a common
saying about former lovers that shows how dramatically
memory can be altered with time. Former golden memories are rewritten to maximize our own self-esteem and to
bring the memories into conformance with our present
beliefs. The fascinating thing about these memory changes
is that the new memories seem so real. Though your logic
tells you that the memories must have been wonderful at
one time or you wouldn't have loved the person so much,
your new beliefs cause a dramatic reinterpretation of the
memories. The more you think about the memories and
re-rehearse them with the new interpretation, the more
they are altered.[4] This is another demonstration of the
amazing creativity of the process we call consciousness. To
preserve our own self-esteem, memory may have to be
drastically altered, yet we feel certain that the revised
version is correct.

These revisionist tendencies can be demonstrated under experimental conditions. In one study[5] high school
students were questioned about their opinions on 30 social
issues, including busing of school children to achieve in-
tegration. The researchers then secretly tried to change the
students' views by having them join small discussion
groups, each of which had a student confederate armed
with very convincing arguments against their known po-

sition. The confederates were highly successful in changing the students' views, with most pro-busing subjects being converted to the anti-busing position. The original anti-busing subjects had their opinions sharply changed in the pro direction. The experimenters then asked the students to recall their earlier stand on busing on the original questionnaire. They reminded them of the previous questionnaire and told them that they would be checking the accuracy of their recall. Control subjects were able to recall accurately their earlier opinion but the students whose views had been changed all *remembered incorrectly that their new position was the same as they had expressed before.* Their memory of their previous opinion was apparently not very strong because it was one item out of 30. Their new and stronger belief on the busing issue caused them to assume that they must have previously answered in agreement with this belief. *Beliefs, logically deduced by the self, can easily be mistaken for actual memories.*

One study of voters who had changed party affiliation from 1972 to 1976 found that 91% reported that they *hadn't* changed parties. Memory, like perception, is creatively distorted to create order and consistency. Whenever we change our beliefs we often also unconsciously change our memories because much of memory recall is actually creative reconstruction.

Elizabeth Loftus, a University of Washington psychology professor, has done hundreds of experiments to show how memory can be intentionally manipulated after the fact. In one such experiment she showed the subjects a series of slides of a car accident in which a car turns right at an intersection with a *yield sign* and hits a pedestrian in the crosswalk. Immediately afterward, she planted a false memory in half of the subjects by asking them, "Did another car pass the red Datsun while it was stopped at the *stop sign*?" When questioned later *over 80%* of that group claimed that they had seen a stop sign rather than a yield sign.

If you have ever been in a courtroom where there are several eyewitnesses to the same event you have probably seen this effect in action. As the memories are rehearsed and reinforced by lawyers, people get more and more confident of them whether they are true or not. Police lineups must be carefully selected to prevent false identifications. For example, if there is only one tall redheaded man in the lineup, he may look so much more like the criminal than the others that he gets selected. Once the witness has picked the same man out of several lineups, the face becomes so familiar that the certainty of identification grows.

Because no one likes to feel like a powerless victim of events, we often unconsciously distort memory to increase our feeling of control. In a famous study of the memories of the children in Chowchilla, California, who in 1976 were kidnapped and buried alive for two days in their school bus, Lenore Terr found that in 1981, 19 of the 26 victims had appended earlier or later events to their memory. Many of these additions were omens which if heeded could have prevented the event. For example, one 8-year-old girl said she had turned down a chance to go camping with her parents that day. Another girl said that she had stepped on a "bad luck square" the day before. One said that a crank caller had called and warned her, though the call had actually occurred afterwards. Five of the children blamed their parents for not reading "the signs" that it was going to happen.

In retelling the story over the years, these added features crept in as a way to "assign meaning to the meaningless." The common feeling of *synchronicity*, where random events seem to be magically related, has the same basis. We look back in time to find relationships whenever something happens to us. If we can relate two events we add order and meaning to our lives. Often this tidying up is done later in the retelling of an event by slightly altering one of the events to make it fit. Once this is done the fit between the two events gets better and better each time we retell it. Just as we creatively fill in our visual blind spot to create order, the same perceptual process fills in and modifies memory.

THE CHALLENGER DISASTER

At 11:00 AM in January of 1986 the space shuttle Challenger exploded on takeoff, killing the entire crew and an elementary teacher along for the ride. The next morning Ulric Neisser gave a questionnaire to 106 students in a Psychology 101 class. They were asked to record where they were when it happened, who else was there, how they felt, and other details. Two and a half years later, 44 of the students still available were given the same questionnaire. The results dramatically confirmed that even apparently vivid memories may be unreliable.

For example, compare the following two accounts given by one student:

NEXT DAY: I was in my religion class and some people walked in and started talking about [it]. I didn't know any details except that it had exploded and the schoolteacher's students had all been watching which I thought was so sad. Then after class I went to my room and watched the TV program talking about it and I got the details from that.

2 1/2 YEARS LATER: When I first heard about the explosion I was sitting in my freshman dorm room with my roommate and we were watching TV. It came on the news flash and we were both totally shocked. I was really upset and I went upstairs to talk to a friend of mine and then I called my parents.

Asked for 5-point confidence ratings on all of the above points the subject gave a top rating of 5. Generally the students' confidence ratings had practically no correlation to the accuracy of their reports. Since the original questionnaire was simply passed out at the end of class, only 11 of the subjects even remembered filling it out. When they were shown their original questionnaires in their own handwriting, many found it hard to believe that their memories could be so wrong. "Whoa! That's totally different from how I remember it" was one comment. Others said, "I still think of it as the other way around" and "I mean, like I told you, I have no recollection of it at all."

It is interesting to try to analyze the kinds of modifications that were made. There was a tendency to remember first seeing it while watching television, probably because the increased drama when they actually saw it on television left more of an impression. Some of the false memories were simply stereotyped fantasies. For example, one girl who heard the news in the cafeteria and got so sick she couldn't finish her lunch said the second time that she was in her dorm room and a girl came running down the hall screaming, "The space shuttle just blew up."

Another one remembered the second time that she heard it when she was home with her parents.

Before anything was said about the accuracy of the second questionnaires, several memory recovery techniques were used in an attempt to improve the accuracy of recall. Subjects were asked to think of additional ways that they *might* have heard the news, to change their perspective, recall the emotional context, and finally they were even shown their original questionnaire. None of the techniques had any effect at all. The experimenters commented: "As far as we can tell the original memories are just gone."

MODULAR MEMORY

Thinking and memory are impossible to separate. The same reinforcement of synapses that causes modules of thinking to form is also the basis of memory. It is not surprising therefore to find that memory is also organized as many separate specialized modules. New categories, called schemas, are created as needed in a way that makes each individual's memory organization unique. Memory organization also has critical decision points where a new category may or may not be created. Each decision point (bifurcation as it is called in chaos theory) affects future memory abilities and also the course of future development. Your unique pattern of aptitudes and abilities are strongly affected by minor external influences at these critical times.

Each person has a unique pattern of memory abilities: good in some areas and bad in others. A person may have a terrible memory for names and faces, yet have an excellent memory for places and numbers. Each specialized kind of memory is independent. Some musical conductors can effortlessly memorize an entire score and yet have a difficult time remembering where their car is parked.

BRAIN DAMAGE EVIDENCE

Brain damage resulting from strokes (death of a small area of the brain) or injury can cause loss of very specific categories of memory while preserving others. Though each brain seems to have its own unique organization and there is little correlation of exact location for memory types, we can learn much about the organization of memory from these cases. For example, some bilingual people have lost one language yet retained another, which would indicate that they have separate structures in different parts of the brain for each language. Others lose the ability to recognize faces while continuing to have normal vision and ability to recognize other objects. Some people lose the ability to recognize words representing concrete objects like *acorn*, *needle*, and *goose* but have no problem with abstract words like *arbiter*, *pact*, and *supplication*. Others have the reverse pattern, retaining concrete words and losing the abstract words. In one reported case the patient lost the ability to recognize things distinguished primarily by looks (e.g., plants, animals) but had no problem with items distinguished by how you use them (e.g., tools, household objects).[6] Even specific categories can be quite separate: One person, with a hobby of gardening, lost the ability to recognize flowers while retaining the ability to recognize all other things.[7] Parts of the human body seem to have their own separate memory structure, as there are many reports of separate loss of body-related words. One patient lost only the verbal ability to recognize animals by name.[8] He did fine with inanimate things and was accurate when presented with a picture of an animal, but he couldn't describe the same animal after hearing its name. Other recognition categories that have been observed to be separate modules include tools, animal and food items, numerals, and musical instruments. Clearly, the recognition process is the result of a large number of specialists working in parallel. These specialist modules organize spontaneously and evolve uniquely for individuals according to their needs and experiences.

Conduction aphasia demonstrates how the ability to remember literally exactly what was said is separate from the ability to recall meaning. The patients seem to have normal abilities to speak and understand fluently and intelligently, yet they are unable to repeat back word for word arbitrary sequences of words even two words long. They also cannot repeat back verbatim sentences of more than a few words. Though they are unaware of doing it, they will radically paraphrase the sentence, preserving only the meaning.

PARALLEL MEMORY STRUCTURES

Different contexts and viewpoints are examined in parallel by different parts of the brain so that, for example, if you can't recognize a banana by its shape, then perhaps you can by color. Shapes are recognized through self-organized modules that form near the part of the brain where various shape-sensing outputs of the eye are mapped to the brain. Color recognition is through another module formed near the color-sensing map to the brain.

People can be recognized by their face, voice, accent, posture, walk, clothes, name, location, or even the time we met them. Although each of these traits probably represents a separate module, recognition often requires only a strong match from one of them. Overall, the act of recognition is the sum total of all of these strategies. Just as a color print is built up from the sum total of many separate images, each a different color, our recognition is based on many different strategies used together. The final result, however, is probably the result of the same kind of competitive mechanism that selects the most confident module to control speech or movement.

The timing of an event seems to be remembered by a separate structure than the one that remembers the event itself. This is demonstrated by certain types of brain damage where things are remembered but the order in which they occurred is forgotten. Emotional feelings associated with an event seem to be likewise remembered separately. Some people lose the ability to remember preferences. The title of a book or movie is clearly remembered in a different module from the plot in my brain. I know this because I can often remember the story in detail, yet forget its title or author.

EXPLAINING VERSUS DOING

Verbal or declarative memory, which allows us to explain how to do something, is completely separate from the memory of how we actually do it. Although we certainly remember how to speak, walk, or swallow, we can't explain verbally how to do them because it was never useful to learn them that way. If we become a throat specialist we will probably learn a parallel verbal memory of how to swallow, which will allow us to analyze and explain it. Just as our self maintains memories that form a belief system for explaining our unconsciously controlled behavior, it also may learn to analyze and discuss movements and other unconsciously controlled procedures. Memories that actually control the behaviors and movements are completely separate.

Advertisers have become experts in directing their message to your subconscious behavior modules. When you make a purchase, it often conflicts with what your self would logically choose. Of course, the self is a master of rationalization, so it will probably make up a plausible story to explain the purchase. For example, the sales of Ford Broncos skyrocketed after O. J. Simpson was televised nationwide driving his. The buyers would probably tell you that they bought it because they liked the styling or the quality but most would be angry if you pointed out the Simpson connection.

Numerous experiments have demonstrated that we can create subliminal knowledge by, for example, flashing words for such a brief time duration that they don't enter consciousness. Later testing will then show an increased preference for the words even though the subjects claim that they never saw them. This is not surprising at all when we consider the parallel and modular nature of memory. Learning obviously occurred in some module even though the stimulus was too short to enter consciousness.

With practice, you can improve your memory for a particular kind of thing. Actors, for example, can develop an amazing ability to memorize long scripts though their recall for other things may remain average. Dancers develop the ability to remember long movement sequences, but this has no effect on their ability to memorize verbal scripts. A restaurant maître d' can learn to recognize thousands of patrons' faces and names but may not be able to memorize dance movements. Each of these memory abilities develops independently because each is a separate module in the brain.

One of the important flaws in the self-concept taught by our society is a distorted idea of the certainty and unity of our memory. By understanding the illusions and limitations of our memory, we can avoid many conflicts and begin to know ourselves and others better.

CHAPTER FIVE

Other Concepts of Self

Man can be defined as the animal that can say "I,"
that can be aware of himself as a separate entity.
—— Erich Fromm, 1955

We all have a self-concept that we have learned from our parents, teachers, and society. This important mental software defines our experience of consciousness, our abilities, and our potential for happiness. It is so basic to our being that it is hard for us to imagine just how different the experience of consciousness is to other people in other places and other times.

Our self-concept is a collection of basic beliefs about consciousness and the nature of reality.[1] These beliefs define our conscious experience at such a basic level that our experience will always convincingly confirm them, even when they conflict with objective reality.

Study the list in Table I and try to imagine how your consciousness and your life would be changed if you could change each belief to the opposite of what it is now. Your culture and your family have taught you one of the variations of each belief, but there are people in the world who strongly disagree with you on every one of them. These people are as certain that they are right as you are because

TABLE I
Self-Concept Beliefs

My destiny is controlled by myself/gods.

I imagine reality/it exists and I simply experience it.

Time flies/is not significant.

I can/cannot use introspection to see the workings of my mind.

I can/cannot see visual imagery, calling up pictures in my mind.

I can think in words/gods speak to me.

All/some of my thoughts are in words.

I am naturally lucky/unlucky.

I am naturally healthy/unhealthy.

I am basically a good/bad person.

Life is beautiful/horrible.

I am sensitive/insensitive to pain.

My mind is singular/a collection of modules.

I primarily strive for my self/nuclear family/extended family/tribe/company/country.

their conscious experience continually confirms their belief just as convincingly as yours does.

The gap-filling mechanism of our brain uses these beliefs as the model for interpreting reality. *Consciousness will creatively construct our reality in a way that will make it fit the expectations of our beliefs.* If we believe that we are controlled by gods, we will interpret everything that happens to us that way and, thanks to our gap-filling ability, it will seem convincing and consistent. Likewise, if we believe that our self module alone controls our actions and our destiny, then that interpretation of reality will seem convincingly correct.

FIGURE 6. This drawing of an old hag can also be seen as a beautiful girl looking away and to the left. Note:The hag's nose is the girl's chin, her mouth is the girl's necklace. Either belief is convincingly confirmed by your perception. (Reprinted with the permission of Scribner/a Lisa Drew Book, a Division of Simon & Schuster Inc., from *The Modular Brain* by Richard M. Restak, M.D.)

Perception tries to make sense out of reality by stretching it to fit our beliefs. When it succeeds, the feeling of certainty can be very deceptive. For example, looking at Figure 6 you may see an old hag or a beautiful woman, but once your mind has clicked into one interpretation, that one seems very convincing. With a little effort you can change your belief to the other interpretation and then, with some practice, that one will seem certain. (Note that the hag's nose can be the beauty's chin, her mouth a necklace.) This false feeling of certainty is a basic characteristic of the mind. A belief becomes a template for making sense of the world, and, once we fill in properly to make an interpretation work, it feels convincingly like the only possible one.

The basic assumptions of our self-concept can be dead wrong and yet appear to be obviously right. The good news is that, just like our interpretation of Figure 6, our assumptions can be changed. With practice a new version of consciousness will click into place and feel natural. People used to regard of earth as the center of the universe. Our concept of the self module as the center of our mental universe is just as false. Learning to see the self module as a member of a team of specialists instead of the whole team can go a long way toward improving our understanding of ourselves and others.

Many of the self-concept beliefs in Table I can be considered modern "inventions" that have never been tried before and still have not spread to primitive societies. For example, our belief that we can directly control our own destiny and the idea that we can look into our own thoughts with introspection are both probably less than 5000 years old.[2] Both strongly affect the very nature of the conscious experience.

THE SELF IN OTHER CULTURES

Our concept of the self seems to us so obvious that it is hard to appreciate that most of the population of the world today would find it quite bizarre. Other cultures base their consciousness on entirely different assumptions. Our sense of time, which includes continual progress and change, and our narrow boundaries of self, only loosely linked to family and community, are incomprehensible to most of the world.

Paul Heelas and Andrew Lock of the University of Lancaster in England have made an extensive study of the anthropology of the self-concept[3] in indigenous cultures. They analyzed eight different cultures and made a chart (Figure 7) plotting where each stood on the first two beliefs listed in Table 1. Belief that the self is in control of reality can exist in varying degrees, so they made a graph with the horizontal axis representing where that culture's belief lies: Complete self-control of reality is on the left, and no control (reality controlled by gods) is on the right. The vertical axis represents the degree of internalization of reality, with the bottom extreme meaning that all reality exists only in the imagination and the top indicating completely objective reality. As Figure 7 shows, each culture has a unique combination of these basic assumptions. This creates a unique mentality and experience of consciousness.

The Tibetan Buddhist mystics, in the lower left corner, represent an extreme of internalization and self in control. They taught that

> ... the world and all phenomena which we perceive are but
> mirages born from our imagination ...
> They emanate from the mind
> And into the mind they sink.

At the other extreme, in the upper right corner, are the Dinka people, who live along the White Nile in Africa and

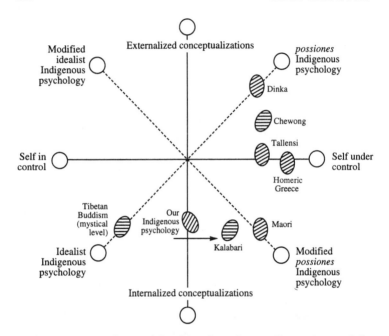

FIGURE 7. Heelas and Lock's plot of two dimensions of the self-concepts of eight different cultures studied: degree of self-control and degree of internalization. (Reprinted with the permission of Academic Press, San Diego, from *Indigenous Psychologies: The Anthropology of the Self* by Paul Heelas and Andrew Lock.)

essentially have no concept of a mind. As Godfrey Lienhardt[4] described it,

> The Dinka have no conception which at all closely corresponds to our popular modern conception of the "mind" as mediating and, as it were, storing up the experiences of the self. There is for them no such interior entity to appear, on reflection to stand be-

tween the experiencing self at any given moment and what is or has been an exterior influence upon the self.

The idea of having a mind seems so obvious and real to us. Yet it is simply a concept, one not shared by all people.

The traditional Maori culture of New Zealand has another way of experiencing reality.[5] They believe themselves to be descended from their gods, so a man's inheritance of the supernatural qualities, *mana* and *tapu*, determines his position in society. *Mana* is a variable quantity given and taken by the gods. As *mana* increases, so does the success of the person. The *tapu* is a state of sacredness that has to be maintained by properly observing complex rules and rituals. *Mana* will increase only if the *tapu* is kept clear. They conceptualize most emotions as being associated with specific organs of the body, so the self is essentially split up into these separate organs, which at various times take control. The self is thus an observer rather than a controller of experience. If you had been raised since birth in the traditional Maori culture, your experience of consciousness and reality would be as we have just described: It would seem as obvious and natural to you as your own self-concept does now.

THE CONCEPT OF TIME

Our concept of time is another dimension of the basic mental software that defines our experience of consciousness. Again, we are out of step with most of the people of the world. Though our sense of fast-flowing time and change seems very natural to us, it is uniquely an invention of modern culture. The majority of the world's population is born into a tribal or peasant environment where one's life is pretty much a repetition of the life of one's parents. Time takes on a completely different meaning under these conditions. There is no such thing as progress, so each year is basically like the one before. The yearly cycle of the seasons endlessly repeats itself and provides a comforting familiarity.

The Trobriand Islanders of the South Pacific were extensively studied by Bronislaw Malinowski.[6] Their sense of time represents an extreme case in that *the concept of time is virtually nonexistent*; their language and their way of thinking are constructed in a way that essentially ignores time. They have no word for "to be" nor do they have a word for "to become"; existence is implied by the names for things, as are the current state they are in. When a thing changes, its name also changes. For example, the *taytu* is a species of yam that they grow. The single word *taytu* implies that a perfectly ripe and well-formed specimen is present now. If the *taytu* isn't at harvesting ripeness, it is not a *taytu*. If it is unripe it is called a *bwanawa*. If it is overripe it is called a *yowana*. If it is blighted it becomes a *nukunokuna*. If it has a rotten patch it is called a *taboula*. If misshapen it is a *usasu*. If perfect in shape but small, it is a *yagogu*. A postharvest gleaning is called a *ulumadala*.

> When the spent tuber, the yowana, sends its shoots underground, as we would put it, it is not a yowana with shoots but a *silisata*. When new tubers have formed on these shoots, it is not a silisata but a *gadena*.

> An object cannot change an attribute and retain its identity.

> Trobriand verbs are timeless, making no temporal distinctions. History and mythical reality are not the past to the Trobriander. They are forever present, participating in all current being, giving meaning to all activities and all existence. A Trobriander will speak of the garden which his mother's brother planted, or the one which the mythical Tudava planted, in exactly the same terms with which he will refer to the garden which he himself is planting now; and it will give him satisfaction to do so.

They have no word for "to be" or for "to become" because they have no concept of time. Remember, the self module, as we define it, is the module that does introspection and talks about our thoughts. It is not surprising that the structure of language has such a strong influence on one's self-concept.

The Trobrianders do not value change. They expect things to stay the same next year as they are this year. This was a big problem for the pearl traders who tried to get them to work. Nicely made European tools[7] that seemed far superior to the crude tools they made themselves had no attraction for the Trobrianders. We Westerners are so accustomed to desiring change, progress, and improvement that we find it difficult to understand people wanting to keep things the way they are. The Amish people in Pennsylvania have an attitude toward change that is similar to the Trobriander attitude.

Our society's concept of time has been created by advertising and the imperatives of a consumer society. It has made us feel anxious for progress and therefore has profoundly affected our material wealth. The unfortunate side effect is that many people have lost the ability to enjoy the moment and feel trapped in a rat race. Happiness and contentment may not be compatible with maximum material progress.

PAIN: A LEARNED CONCEPT

Pain feels convincingly like an inherent thing wired into our nervous system and not affected by beliefs. Yet there is much evidence that it is as changeable as our sense of time. When a hypnotist suggests that we will feel no pain, we can tolerate pins stuck into our arms and even surgery without being bothered by the pain. What the hypnotist does is make us *believe* that we won't be bothered by the pain, and, as a result, our perception of the pain changes to something benign.

Experiments have shown that a pain reduction equal to that achieved under hypnosis can be achieved without hypnosis if the subjects are given brief instruction on pain-reducing strategies. By simply relaxing and diverting attention, an 80% reduction in pain[8] can be achieved by most people. Acupuncture creates an alternate focus and a rationale for experiencing reduced pain that is very effective if you believe. When a fakir or yoga lies on a bed of nails he simply puts aside the sensation of pain.

We all learn how to interpret pain from our culture, and it becomes a part of our self-concept. The Sherpa of Nepal traditionally act as porters for mountain climbers who climb Mount Everest. They uncomplainingly carry

77-pound packs up the mountain with little outerwear, even in freezing temperatures. Their culture takes pride in the ability to endure pain and hardship without flinching. Despite years of training and conditioning, our climbers tell of great hardships even with their hi-tech thermal wear, oxygen, and minimal packs.

In 1982 two American psychologists[9] performed a series of controlled experiments on six Nepalese and five Western trekkers. They found that the Nepalese were just as sensitive to stimulus as the Westerners and just as able to make discriminations between high- and low-intensity stimuli. The only difference was found to be in the interpretation of painful stimuli: What the Westerners would call unbearable pain, the Sherpas would accept stoically. Their concept of pain is simply different from ours.

In Bavaria today it is considered inappropriate to ask for anesthesia when you have a tooth filled, yet 200 miles to the north most Germans consider it a necessity. Many African tribes painfully mutilate their bodies without complaint. Dentists will confirm that even within a single culture, people's tolerance for pain varies greatly.

It is common for people with serious injuries who are absorbed in important survival actions not to feel the pain until they are safe and able to focus on the pain. In wartime, soldiers often suffer severe wounds, including loss of limbs and open abdominal wounds, without complaining about the pain. Some soldiers with major injuries actually react with euphoria at the thought of being able to leave the battlefield and go home. In Lamaze natural childbirth classes mothers are taught to ignore or positively experience the pain of childbirth. Many can then deliver without anesthesia.

Noise above a certain threshold is perceived as pain. One of the best possible demonstrations of the effect of mental attitude on pain can be seen at a heavy metal rock concert. The teenage fans love what would seem quite painful to an older person or even a young lover of classical music. Outdoor rock concerts often have complaints that the noise is intolerable from annoyed residents who live miles away. The insignificant noise of a dripping water faucet can be agonizing if your mental attitude makes it so.

Reactions to heat and cold are also largely determined by learned concepts. The aboriginal people of Tierra del Fuego close to the antarctic circle lived essentially naked in the freezing cold when the Europeans first encountered them. People who live in cold climates rejoice at unseasonably warm winter weather and remove their coats when the temperature reaches 40 degrees. In the deserts of north Africa tribesmen live with average summer high temperatures of over 110 degrees. Hypnotic suggestion can make people feel uncomfortably hot or cold in a comfortable room by simply making them *believe* it is hot or cold.

If you work on your own attitude toward pain, heat, and cold, you can make significant changes in your own reactions. By practicing a kind of positive thinking when you are exposed to these stimuli, you can learn to increase your tolerance significantly. The secret is to imitate your friends who say, "I love heat!" and also to imitate the ones who say, "I love cold!" With practice you can change your beliefs until you really do feel comfortable over a wide temperature range. By widening your comfort range you can learn to be comfortable when others are miserable and complaining.

THE BOUNDARIES OF SELF

Another part of our self-concept that would seem bizarre to the majority of the people on earth is our shrunken self boundary. The self defends and pursues goals within a conceptual boundary; this boundary is an important component of our self-concept. In most of the world's cultures the self boundary includes at least an extended family and more often a tribe or community (Figure 8). In modern American culture the tendency has been for more and more people to shrink this boundary to a single person: themselves. All goals then become personal goals, and the lines of defense end with the limits of your own body. When we move far away from home we are hurting the extended family to benefit our narrower self-concept.

One of the reasons the Japanese were able to overtake the West economically so rapidly in the 1980s was that their self-concept included the company for which they worked. They worked incredibly long hours and did without many comforts in pursuit of goals that were really company goals. Their self boundary included their employer and possibly the whole country. Instead of seeking goals individually, the purpose was to fit into and be useful to the group; the goals were then achieved by the group. Thanks to American television and movies, this is all rapidly changing.

The Asian mentality, in general, tends to place the boundaries of self at least at the extended family level. The family thrives and gains status because each member tries to fit in and be useful. Marriages are arranged with the bride being selected for the good of the family, not the

Boundaries of Self

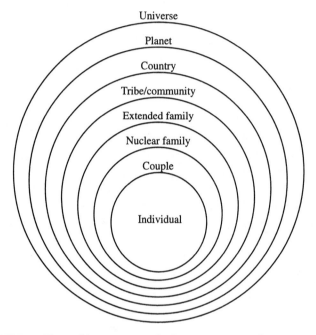

FIGURE 8. The self-concept includes a concept of boundaries which varies between cultures. The narrowest boundary ends at the skin of the individual's body while the widest includes the entire universe.

groom. A Chinese man considers himself a brother, a son, a husband, or a father, but hardly ever just as himself.[10]

The Balinese consider themselves not as individuals but as members of a social category. This is reflected in the way people are named. While we are given a name at birth that is uniquely ours and stays with us for life, the Balinese names[11] change with changes of status. Infants aren't even given a name until they are 105 days old. That name is used only sporadically until adolescence, when it ceases to be used. More commonly used are kinship names, which one shares with all siblings and cousins within one's generation. There are also names based on birth order: Wayan for the firstborn, Nioman for the second, and so on. An adult who becomes a parent is called "Father of . . . " or "Mother of . . . " followed by the child's name. When a grandchild is born the name changes to "Grandmother of . . . " etc. and similarly when a great-grandchild is born. Public titles are also used for people with jobs such as postman, politician, and so on. Social life in such a society also tends to be less personal, more general and formal. Relationships tend to be seen as links between representatives of different groups or classes.

Property concepts are another way to view the boundaries of self. The nuclear family in the United States ideally is bounded by the property lines of their home. In many parts of the world, these boundaries are not so clear. The Japanese often live in a company compound that includes recreational facilities and even company vacation resorts. The American Indians, and many other tribal and nomadic cultures, have no concept of individual property.

The Dogon people[12] of Mali have permanent villages with a population in the thousands, yet their definition of house is the people living there, not the structure. The Dogon house is never sold and is thought of as belonging to the mythical descendants of the people who occupied the village before the Dogon arrived. For each individual, the village is "his" house; his family simply sleeps in a particular structure. The self boundary in this case could be said to extend to the limits of the village.

The extreme extension of the self boundaries would be found in the teachings of many religions that espouse a universal consciousness. The self boundary would thus include the entire universe. At the other extreme, a fairly common symptom of strokes and right hemisphere brain damage is unilateral neglect: The patient, paralyzed on the left side, denies that his left arm or leg belongs to him.[13] Accustomed to depending upon a—now damaged—module in the right hemisphere to attend to such things, the self module simply narrows the boundaries of self down to the right half of the body. The opposite occurs when an amputee with an artificial arm or leg learns to extend his self boundary out to include the artificial limb.

You can change your own self boundaries by practicing thinking of yourself as a part of something greater than yourself. Your individual cells are born and die as part of a continual cooperative process that you lump together and call your body. Your body in turn is a component part of many processes that are larger than you: your family, your community, job, country, the earth ecosystem, and even the universe. Life can seem richer and death less important with these expanded concepts of self.

THE SELF-CONCEPT IN HISTORY

The major turning points in the history of mankind can all be related to changes in the self-concept. These changes are easy to trace at the start of the Renaissance because the books of this era are full of discussions of the new concepts (see Table II). Earlier history is not so clear because our ability to translate ancient hieroglyphics, cuneiform, and other written languages is limited to simple concrete meanings. The first major work in a language that we can translate with some certainty is the *Iliad*. This epic story was developed about 1230 BC, verbally passed on by Greek bards and then written down by Homer about 850 BC. With the exception of a few speeches, believed to be added later,[14] there is no indication of consciousness in any of the 24 books. The concept of will, though highly developed in Plato's time, does not appear. Actions are driven not by conscious plans, reasons, or motives but by actions or speeches of the gods.

By 399 BC the concept of free will had evolved to the point that Socrates demonstrated the meaning of the concept of self in control by making a conscious decision to intentionally wait for his sentence of poisoning though he ironically submits to the will of others. Plato dramatized it in *Phaedo* as follows:

> . . . since the Athenians thought it right to condemn me, I have thought it right and just to sit here and to submit to whatever sentence they may think fit to impose. For by the dog of Egypt, I think that these muscles and bones would long ago have been in Megara or Boeotia, prompted by their opinion of what is best, if I had not thought it better and more honorable to submit to whatever penalty the state inflicts, rather than escape by flight.

The Athenians accomplished great things with their newly discovered idea of a self in control. However, their self-concept still didn't include introspection. "Know thyself," inscribed on the Delphic oracle in about 600 BC,

TABLE II
Issues of Selfhood in Different Historical Eras.[a]

Historical era	Self-knowledge, self conception	Self-definition	Fulfillment	Relation of individual to society
Late medieval	Unproblematic Increase sense of unity of single life	Mortality and virtue Honor, glory, reputation (fixed criteria) Otherwise, society defined identity: rank, kin, etc.	Christian salvation (in heaven) (Possible) public acclaim	"Great Chain of Being"—fixed, stable order Self equated with social, public self
Early modern (16th to 18th century)	Unproblematic for own self; for others, question of inner *true* self vs. outer *apparent* self Increased interest in individuality, uniqueness of self	Concept of personal change, development Sincerity; equivalence of inner and outer selves, as a virtue Loss of identity through family lineage	Christian salvation Incipient secular fulfillment, as in creativity	Unstable (social mobility) Some separation (privacy)
Puritan	Self-consciousness Concern with self-deception (henceforth, self-knowledge uncertain)	In principle, none! (predestination)	Christians salvation; but individual is helpless Inner struggle to overcome sin and weakness	Work: Success means salvation
Romantic (late 18th, early 19th centuries)	Need to discover own destiny and fulfill it (duty) Imperial, *hypertrophied* self	Individual exists prior to particular social roles Quest for fulfillment as self-definition Personality as identity	Creativity Passion ("romantic" love) Thus, grope for secularized concept of fulfillment	Individual vs. society struggle for freedom Individual inseparable from society, but can change roles

Victorian (mid and late 19th century)	Repression, hypocrisy Involuntary self-disclosure Imperial, "hypertrophied" self	Self-reliance, rugged individualism Adolescence as crisis in self-definition	Seek fulfillment alone (transcendentalism) Private, family life is paramount	Peaceful coexistence (transcendentalism) Change society (Progressivism, Utopianism)
Early 20th century	Devaluation of self Impossibility of complete self-knowledge (Freud)	Socioeconomic status Existential concerns, authenticity Personality, social skills Radical choice	Society prevents fulfillment (alienation) Emotional fulfillment in family Work as unfulfilling	Hostile, critical, muckraking Alienation
Recent 20th century	Belief in personal uniqueness Values of self-exploration	Personality Socioeconomic status	Quest for celebrity Quest for means of self-actualization	Accommodation Myth-making

aFrom "How the self became a problem: A psychological review of historical research," *Journal of Personality and Social Psychology*, 1987, Volume 52, No. 1, p. 164, by Roy F. Baumeister.

sounds to us like a reference to introspection. However, in the context of the mentality of the time[15] the meaning was probably more related to knowing your talents and capacities so that you could carry out your duties effectively and with good judgment.

A thorough search through medieval literature by R. W. Hanning of Yale University[16] found virtually no reference to inner struggles. Though Saint Augustine wrote, "In the inner man dwells truth," he also wrote, "No person should therefore desire to change his or her station, any more than a finger should wish to be the body's eye" ("station" here means standing in society). The Christian writings on salvation prior to the 12th century speak only of collective salvation. After that time, the idea of final judgment developed and with it came a concept of each person's being held accountable for one's acts.

The first literature with significant references to the internal self was by Petrarch, a 14th century Italian poet. He was one of the first to rediscover Plato and other Greek teachings as the basis of a new cultural framework. As these ideas spread, the result was the dramatic change in the self-concept, which resulted in the Renaissance in Europe. Rene Descartes' famous "I think, therefore I am" in 1644 showed the further development and spread to France of the concepts of introspection and the individual self.

The literature and drama in the time of Shakespeare exhibits plenty of internal conflict. Hamlet's famous "To be or not to be" is the kind of internal dialogue that was absent from medieval literature. "The fault, dear Brutus, is not in our stars, but in ourselves" reflects clearly the concept of self-control of destiny. In Greek tragedy, circumstances rather than personality are the central focus. Oedipus' personality is irrelevant to his misfortunes, which were decreed by fate.

Biographies were practically unheard of in the Middle Ages because the idea of the individual self was not part of the mentality. People thought of themselves only as a member of a larger group. During the late 18th century, individual personality came to be increasingly valued, even above social rank. Biographies became a popular form. When people wrote about their travels, they began to talk about their personal feelings and what moved them. Before this time, travel descriptions focused on general information depicting the place from an impartial viewpoint. Boswell's travel descriptions are extremely personal, revealing as much about his own feelings as about the place he describes.

With the narrowing of self boundaries has come an increasing emphasis on privacy and individual rights. In pre-18th century French towns, unmarried people accused of fornication, cuckolds, and men who had done women's work were subjected to the charivari. Noisy public ridicule was the punishment for things that would today be considered private family matters. Even kings were never left alone. Servants were ever-present in rich families, and the poor families lived together in a single room, often sharing a single bed. Until the end of the 17th century nobody expected to be left alone.[17] With the trend toward individualization came the idea of separate rooms and servants' halls. The private chair was introduced at the dinner table to replace the bench. The continuation of this trend in modern times has led to each family desiring its own fenced yard for privacy and a private bedroom for each child.

Too much logic and self-control can to some degree rob life of the richness of the senses. In the late 18th century a reaction began against the extreme Rationalism of the previous century. The Romantic era emphasized individual feelings and fulfillment. Artists, natives, and peasants were idealized for their direct, simple approach to life. In 1798 William Wordsworth wrote,

One Impulse from a vernal wood
May teach you more of man
Of moral evil and of good
Than all the sages can.

The Romantic versus Rationalist dichotomy is an important part of our self-concept that strongly affects our perception of reality. Rapid changes in popular culture show how quickly these basic concepts can change and how easily influenced most people are by the society in which they live.

In the 1960s there was a brief revival of romanticism when frilly clothes, simple folk songs, and Rod McKuen poetry became mass market hits. Ten years later, the pendulum had swung back, making these same songs, poems, and styles seem cloyingly sweet and embarrassing. This rapid change in our basic way of perceiving things illustrates just how quickly our mental software can change. The same things that previously brought pleasure can become an embarrassment as the underlying concepts that shape our reality are changed.

The important thing is to recognize that since our mind creatively constructs our reality around self-concept beliefs, these beliefs will *always* seem to be obviously true. The mind interprets and fills in as necessary to confirm them no matter what they are. Once the beliefs that constitute our self-concept are planted in our minds in early childhood, they tend to grow stronger with every year because they seem to be continually confirmed by experience. Only with great mental effort can we use our logic to see past these mental illusions and find and correct the errors in our self-concept.

CHAPTER SIX

False Beliefs

*A belief is a perceptual framework which leads us
to see the world in a way that reinforces that framework.*
—— *Edward De Bono, 1990*

The greatest deception men suffer is from their own opinions.
—— *Leonardo da Vinci, c. 1500*

*We are so constituted that we believe the most incredible things;
and, once they are engraved upon the memory,
woe to him who would endeavor to erase them.*
—— *Goethe, 1771*

False beliefs are always something *somebody else* has. Yet everywhere beliefs are in conflict. People even die for and endure torture for their beliefs. We cling to false beliefs steadfastly because of the way perception works: The same filling-in process that helps us to make sense of our world also prevents us from knowing if our beliefs are false. Our mind creatively interprets all of our perceptions in an attempt to fit them to our beliefs and expectations. It is not surprising then that *even false beliefs appear to be convincingly confirmed*. This flaw in our mental makeup has been the source of much strife throughout history.

Positive feedback[1] is an engineering term meaning feedback in the *same* direction. It tends to reinforce and *increase* errors, usually resulting in drastic instability. (Another confusing use of the term *positive feedback* means giving encouragement, which is *not* what we mean here.) A simple example of feedback is the thermostat in your home, which is normally connected to give negative feedback to stabilize the temperature by turning on the heat if it is too cold or the air conditioning if it is too hot. If you reversed the connections to the thermostat so that it would turn on the heat when it got too hot and the air conditioning when it got too cold, that would be positive feedback. The result would be disastrous: If your house started out warm, the furnace would go on and make it hotter and hotter; if it started out cold, the air conditioning would come on, making it colder and colder. Clearly, positive feedback is to be avoided.

Our belief system is a perfect example of positive feedback because *the observations used to test for truth are altered in the direction that is assumed to be true.* The result is a tendency to *lock in on whatever is first assumed to be true.*[2] If we grow up thinking that a flat Earth is the center of the universe, we will see that belief confirmed everywhere we look. This circularity of our belief system makes our world appear much more orderly than it really is. Unfortunately, it also causes much disorder because of the conflicts that result when people begin with different assumptions.

WHY WE HAVE WARS

Wars most always occur between two groups of people who have strong negative beliefs about each other. With time, positive feedback strengthens these beliefs to a breaking point. If you are raised a Catholic in Northern Ireland, then you likely believe that the British are not to be trusted. Generous acts of reconciliation are seen as tricks to gain advantage. In fact, tricks against the British are seen as smart and necessary to prevent the British from gaining first advantage. If an IRA bomb kills schoolchildren, it is seen by true believers as a British trick to make the IRA look bad.[3]

The U.S. involvement in Somalia in 1994 is another example of how negative beliefs can make people see the most generous acts in an evil light. The 20,000 soldiers we unselfishly sent there to help a famine were showered with rocks by children, shot at by snipers, and dragged dead through the streets by exultant citizens of the capital. In the end 42 Americans were killed and 175 wounded before we finally made our hasty retreat. Hatred can distort perception until the most generous acts look like an imperialist plot.

Prejudice between racial groups and sexes is also perpetuated by the circularity of beliefs: If you believe that blacks are criminals and you hear about a crime in your neighborhood just after you saw a black person on your street, it will likely confirm your belief, even though he was innocent. You may read in the paper a week later that a white criminal was caught, but the reinforcement of your belief system is already done and will not be undone by this "exception." In fact, since memory recall is also creatively distorted to fit beliefs, it wouldn't be unusual for someone still to say, "Every time I see a black person in the neighborhood somebody gets robbed." Both perception and memory are naturally distorted to confirm beliefs, regardless of whether they are false or true.

The circularity of belief systems is just as serious when blacks adopt a white conspiracy belief. This makes them interpret all bad events as being caused intentionally by whites. Rudeness of a white clerk in a store is interpreted as prejudice, even though whites are often rude to each other. Drug addiction, AIDS, and high murder rates are seen as results of a white conspiracy. Most wars are a result of this kind of interaction between two false belief systems. Each side thinks it is seeing convincing confirmation of its beliefs. Positive feedback tends to produce instability; when *two* related but distinct positive feedback systems interact, the result can be catastrophic.

Habitual criminals are caught in this kind of cycle. They see the system as an unfair and cruel conspiracy against them, and the citizens and police expect more criminal behavior, so both sides clearly see and get the result they expect. The Communists believed a conspiracy of capitalists was the cause of all of their problems. They could convincingly see confirmation everywhere they looked and honestly believed they were doing the right thing by overthrowing the system. It is now clear that they were wrong, but the world could have been saved a lot of trouble if they had stood back and seen the dangerous circularity of their beliefs.

Another serious problem caused by positive feedback is that it prevents beliefs from changing even when the conditions that originally caused them have rendered them false. Communism survived long after it was obviously not working as well as the free market system. It was born in an age of worker oppression but continued well after unions and government regulations brought exploitation under control in the democratic countries. Distorted perceptions continued to reinforce the now false belief system. Most labor unions were started to protest intolerable wages and working conditions. Once the antimanagement belief was established it became self-perpetuating, even after workers gained control. Many U.S. industries have been destroyed by worker demands that went far beyond fairness, demanding featherbedding and salary excesses. Many false beliefs were once true but were perpetuated by positive feedback to continue long after conditions had changed, rendering them false. Most hatred between countries and ethnic groups is based on events that happened generations ago, but positive feedback perpetuates the hatred.

Some countries, such as England, have had stable, honest government for centuries, while others seem to have one corrupt regime after another. The reason for the difference may well have to do with beliefs. When the English have a corruption scandal, they see it as a temporary aberration and proceed to correct it: They believe in, and expect, good government. In many countries people believe government is always corrupt and develop a way of life based on working around that corruption. These countries are almost impossible to reform because even if the government *is* honest, the people will perceive it as corrupt. Positive feedback keeps them where they started because the initial beliefs are self-perpetuating.

The distortion of perception to confirm beliefs actually has a stabilizing influence on some things. For example, people have a tendency to feel that the place where they grew up is the best of all possible places to live. In Kansas they are glad that they don't have to worry about earthquakes like the poor people in California. Tornadoes and ice storms, on the other hand, are not so bad. If people didn't have this mental trait, California would be even more crowded than it is.

WINNERS AND LOSERS

Most gamblers believe in luck and losing streaks: When they feel lucky they view each successive win as a confirmation of their luck and each loss as an exception. Once the belief turns around to a losing streak, the wins become exceptions. Your personal self-concept can likewise include a belief that you are basically a winner or a loser. In this case the results, in the form of success and happiness, can be profoundly affected by the way life's events are interpreted. A glass half full of water can be seen as half empty. A lost job can be seen as a lucky opportunity to improve or as yet another failure.

A basic part of the mental software of our self-concept includes some basic beliefs about the world. A child reared in a wealthy family may tend to assume that life is easy and anything can be accomplished with a little effort. A totally opposite belief system may result from being raised in a ghetto, welfare-dependent family: The world is hostile and it isn't even worth trying.

The power of beliefs is clearly illustrated by the success of the Jewish immigrants who interpreted the prejudice and hardship they found as a challenge to *try harder*. The same crushing events, interpreted by some ethnic and racial groups as proof that there is no hope, were taken by the Jews as a challenge. The only difference was the initial belief assumption instilled during childhood by the family. Experience is interpreted to confirm beliefs, positive or negative, with often totally opposite results.

Self-esteem is a part of your self-concept defined by your beliefs about your own abilities. If you have high self-esteem you will see your failures as exceptions and always expect success. Some people actually overestimate their abilities and view their own mediocre accomplish-ments as quite exceptional. Low self-esteem can make truly exceptional and talented people see their abilities as mediocre. Again the positive feedback of these distortions of perception tend to perpetuate the initial belief instilled by parents during childhood.

It is quite common to see two brothers or sisters, having grown up in the same family, with a totally opposite view of the family's disposition. One may remember a blissful rela-tionship between the parents, while the other remembers continual bickering. One remembers the parents as loving and supportive, while the other remembers their doling out cruel punishments. Again the reason is positive feedback stemming from a slightly different initial perception of the same family life. Seemingly insignificant events at crucial moments in development can start a child in a negative or positive direction. Once a negative belief is started, percep-tion is distorted to support the negative interpretation of future actions by the parents. This calls for more rebellious and negative behavior, which builds a negative expectation in the parents' minds. Positive feedback soon drives both the parents' and the child's views to extremes by repeatedly confirming what began as a weak initial tendency. Genetic differences between siblings may also be a part of the picture, but positive feedback finishes the job.

DENIAL: IGNORING THE UNTHINKABLE

Denial edits perception by ignoring things that are unpleasant or contrary to our beliefs. It is the antithesis of filling in. We are all in denial of the certainty of our own eventual death. It is a useful defense mechanism that makes life livable by allowing us to ignore things that we are powerless to change. However, it is often misused to allow us to avoid facing realities that could be changed. Denial is simply a special category of false beliefs that edits our reality so that we can unconsciously ignore the unthinkable.

Groups of people unconsciously follow unspoken rules about what can and cannot be discussed. These limits are set by example and are followed without any conscious intent. Abusive or alcoholic parents' problems can go totally unnoticed in families where collective denial is the unspoken rule. Each child maintains a positive belief regarding the parents and actually fails to acknowledge the dysfunctional behavior. Memories that don't fit into the basic belief of a harmonious family are ignored or distorted as long as the belief is sustained. A parent can be alcoholic and the family can shrug it off with an explanation like "Dad is sick again." Once such a family pattern develops,[4] the creative nature of perception and memory makes it seem very natural to continue. In fact, it becomes just as natural as ignoring the blind spot in your vision. Sexual and physical abuse can go on in a family for years and be ignored by everyone. Though the taboo is never actually discussed, everybody knows by example that certain things are taboo subjects.

If you live in a family with sexual or physical abuse, then those unthinkable facts are simply added to your normal denial of death. Patterns of abuse are forgiven and forgotten by pretending they are temporary aberrations. Memories of events are stored away normally, but the retrieval is distorted to agree with the current belief in a perfect family. The person simply avoids thinking about the unpleasant events the same way that he avoids thinking about his own death. However, just as the thought of death sometimes slips through our barrier of denial, other denied thoughts and memories also occasionally flash into consciousness. When beliefs change and denial is allowed to stop, the memories can be reinterpreted to match the new version of reality. "Coming out of the closet" causes all existing memories, previously distorted by the false belief system, to be seen in a new light.

Group pressure seems to be amazingly effective in causing denial of glaringly obvious problems. In Nazi Germany, extermination camps and other atrocities were ignored by almost everyone. People simply failed to see what they could not bear to see. The fact that others were doing the same thing seemed to make it much easier. A sense of loyalty makes it possible to filter perception to an amazing degree.

In failing companies and military campaigns the obvious signs of impending disaster are often ignored by everyone in the managing group. "Groupthink" works by focusing attention on all other possible details except the obvious unpleasant facts. It seems that denial is a contagious disease insofar as the group dynamic arrives at unspoken rules about what is taboo. In the disastrous Bay of Pigs invasion of Cuba and also the Vietnam War, planners blundered ahead in spite of easily available information that would have foretold disaster. The Bay of Pigs invasion was based on the assumption that the Cuban people would unanimously rally to support the 1400 invaders even though a widely circulated poll showed that the vast majority of Cubans supported Castro. In spite of that, nobody thought to ask the CIA, the Secretary of State, or the State Department Cuban desk.[5]

Denial and distortion of reality to match our beliefs are defense mechanisms that make life more tolerable in the short term. However, as the above examples show, in many situations they can exact a high cost in human suffering.

In September of 1919, President Woodrow Wilson had a massive stroke that left him paralyzed and blind on the left side of his body. He also totally neglected the left side of his body, lost his spatial sense, and lost all emotional inflection in his voice. In spite of these handicaps he suffered from denial of symptoms, a common symptom from such strokes. He fired his secretary of state for calling a meeting to discuss the problem. During his last two years in the White House he was severely disabled and couldn't even sit up at his desk or read more than a few lines at a time. Yet he and most of his staff claimed that he was merely lame.[6] He finished the final two years of his term in this severely disabled state and even tried to run for renomination.

Denial is quite common in terminally ill patients and their families. Medical reports and other symptoms seem not to be heard at all. This can be a useful defense for someone in a hopeless situation who is receiving proper treatment. However, denial can be the cause of death when it prevents people with obvious symptoms of cancer or other serious diseases from seeking treatment. Many brain damage patients initially deny serious symptoms like blindness, deafness, paralysis, and loss of memory. Consciousness is extremely creative in perceiving only what it accepts.

When we take a new job, move to a new city, or meet a new friend we often go through a honeymoon period where we are in denial of serious defects. Later, when disillusionment sets in, we can look back at our intact memories of the clear signs of defect amazed that we didn't see them at the time. "Love is blind" because when a person falls in love, he or she has an idealized belief in the other person. Because of this belief, denial causes obvious major faults to go completely unnoticed. Parents often deny the faults of their children, maintaining that a murderer is "a good boy."

In the 1960s Lester Luborsky[7] did some fascinating experiments that demonstrate an ability to censor out undesired visual inputs at the very source. He used a special camera to track a spot of light reflected from the cornea so as to track the scanning eye movements of the subjects as they examined pictures (see Figure 3 for example). He showed the subjects ten pictures and asked them to rate which ones they liked and which they disliked. Three of the pictures had a sexual content. For example, one showed the outline of a woman's breast with a man reading a newspaper in the background. Some of the subjects showed an amazing ability to look at the pictures *without once letting their gaze stray to the sexy part of the picture.*

When they were asked several days later what the pictures were, they remembered little or nothing suggestive about them. It seems that an unconscious module of the mind that controls eye movements is able to protect us from seeing things that violate our standards of acceptability. Selective awareness is a fundamental and necessary part of our brain's function. Without it the world would be a confusing buzz of too many sensations.

THE PLACEBO EFFECT

The placebo effect is a powerful demonstration of the power of beliefs to affect not only our perception but also our immune system. If you have an illness and you believe that something has been done to cure it, you will often either get better or think you have gotten better. Faith healers often have people throw away their crutches after being healed by prayer. Even a sugar pill, called a placebo, will often cure an illness if it is given to you as a cure for that illness.

This effect is so strong that the Food and Drug Administration (FDA) testing procedure for new medications requires an extremely expensive double-blind technique. In a double-blind test half of the test subjects must secretly be given placebos (sugar pills). The results must be tabulated by workers with no knowledge of who got the placebos.

Normally there will always be a considerable number of people who seem to benefit from the treatment. Approval is given only if the drug under test does significantly better than the placebo. The people taking the real medication do better because they get the benefit of the placebo effect plus the effectiveness of the medication.

The other side of the double-blind procedure is the requirement that the researchers must not know which subjects received the real medication. Without this precaution, it has been found that test results will be biased in favor of the new drug. Even though the researchers attempt to be honest, their perception is distorted enough by their belief in the new drug that the results will be tainted if they know who actually got the drug. Subtle errors of perception, ways of asking questions, errors in record keeping, and other factors all have been found to work together to prejudice the results toward confirming the researchers' beliefs.

The double-blind test technique must even be applied to testing new surgery techniques. Dummy surgery is actually performed on some patients in the paid test who are secretly chosen as controls: An incision is made but nothing is done internally. Without this control it is impossible to tell if new surgery really works because patients' symptoms improve even with dummy surgery. The placebo effect is present anytime the patient knows that something was done to improve his condition.

In the Philippines, psychosurgeons perform operations using only their bare hands (and a little palmed chicken blood and guts). Their good results are a testimonial to the power of the placebo effect. Homeopathy is another alternative medical treatment that seems to have no sound scientific basis. Most of the medications are so highly diluted that a typical dose often has *no molecules* of the substance they are supposed to contain.[8] In spite of this fact, the placebo effect causes many people to be highly impressed by the results. Homeopathic drug sales are actually growing by 25% a year.

The opposite of the placebo effect happens when people believe themselves to be unhealthy. The immune system seems to be able to shut down in such situations. Black magic curses actually appear to work by this process. Believing in the power of a voodoo doll with pins in it can make a superstitious person's immune system shut down and put that person in a downward spiral that leads to death. Another common example is the way the survivor in an elderly married couple often dies soon after the partner. A Finnish study of 96,000 widowed people found that their risk of death doubled in the week after their partner's death.[9] Again, positive feedback is a factor, since any illness confirms the belief that death is near. Mental attitude seems to be able to affect not only perception but also the body's immune system.

MENTAL ILLNESS

Positive feedback is also an important factor in mental illness. Beliefs that cause fear can distort perception to reinforce a fear until it becomes absolutely terrifying. The Darwinian competition between modules of the mind for strongest meaning or match makes it possible for a rogue module, which increasingly overreacts to a fear, to develop. A slight fear of flying can intensify with each flight because the fear causes even small bumps, due to turbulence, to seem worse than they really are. As the fear belief grows stronger, the overreaction grows with it.

Binge behavior such as fits of heavy eating, drinking, or gambling could also be examples of a rogue module. The instant change in behavior when a person clicks into the binge state has all the earmarks of a change of modules. The dramatic personality changes of some people when drunk could easily just be the personality traits of their "drunk module." This module has its own developmental history, which is also influenced by the fact that the physiological effects of alcohol are present whenever it is in control. Lost memories of things that happened while drunk may be recovered the next time the person is drunk again.

Depression, also a result of positive feedback, may begin with a real cause, such as a misfortune or a chemical imbalance caused by PMS. The negative experience soon causes even good events to be interpreted in a negative way. The more misfortunes accumulate, the more negative interpretations grow until the person plummets into a deep depression. The negative belief system distorts perception, causing even well-meaning friends' helpful actions to be seen as cruel attacks.

Hypochondria sometimes includes a much-lowered tolerance for pain. Normal feelings can be interpreted as pains once the belief of illness is planted. Normal body sensations that would usually be ignored can take on an ominous significance. The false belief in the illness distorts perception to create the expected symptoms. A large percentage of visits to physicians are found to have no physical basis. Though it is impossible to get accurate figures, estimates of such visits vary from 30 to 80%.[10]

Paranoia, a similar runaway belief system, occurs when any event is interpreted as a personal threat: The phone rings and nobody is there, a stranger standing on the street corner is perceived as somebody keeping a watch on the house, a headline on a newspaper is a hidden message. Once this paranoid belief takes control, distorted perception confirms it, and it grows stronger with each imagined experience. Again, positive feedback reinforces an initially weak belief until it grows stronger and stronger.

FINANCIAL BELIEFS

Financial markets tend to go through wild and destructive cycles of boom and bust that are a result of the same positive feedback of our perceptions. During a bear (down) market, everything tends to be interpreted negatively, including things that would be considered good news in a bull market. A good earnings report becomes bad news—it could mean that the economy will get overheated and cause inflation and a hike in interest rates. In a bull (up) market, that same news would be welcomed as an indication that prosperity is continuing. The explanations given by news reporters for stock average movements, up or down, are often the same, with the interpretation depending on whether the prevailing belief is bullish or bearish.

An unstable stock market oscillates between limits because of positive feedback: Rising prices make people willing to pay more for a stock while falling prices make them want to sell. Interest rate adjustments are the Federal Reserve Board's attempt to add negative feedback to stabilize the system. If things look too good they raise interest rates, which makes people want to sell their stocks.

Interest rates are also strongly affected by the prevailing belief system. Prior to 1966, interest rates were stable at less than 4.5% for decades. By 1973 inflation reached a runaway 36.4%,[11] but the prime rate rose to only 8% because people continued to believe in the stability of the dollar. An investment in treasury bills that year would lose about 20% of its real value. As a result of the negative interest in those years, real interest rates are still incredibly high by pre-1970s standards. People no longer believe, as they used to, that the dollar can remain stable and free from inflation.

The prices of homes also suffer from boom and bust cycles as a result of changing beliefs and expectations. The inflation of the 1970s caused home prices to grow dramatically in many parts of the country. As people learned to expect home prices to double every few years, a kind of frenzy developed, driving prices to ridiculous heights. In many areas, less than 30% of the families could afford the median-priced home. Once this bubble burst, hundreds of thousands of homes were foreclosed as their value fell below the loan balance. The idea of reasonable value for a home is still unreasonably high in some areas because the drop in values is seen as an aberration rather than a return to sanity. The original belief in the wisdom of home ownership is still alive in most people, despite some very negative evidence.

URBAN LEGENDS

Urban legends are the modern version of folklore. They are untrue stories that are picked up by the news media and spread by word of mouth until they take on a life of their own. They are a clear demonstration of the power of positive feedback in that they begin with a single false story and then mushroom into a major epidemic that is nearly impossible to stamp out. Several tabloid newspapers specialize in running this type of story and don't hesitate to make up stories and even fake photographs to fan the flames.

The moon-and-stars trademark used to appear on all Proctor and Gamble products until somebody started a rumor that the company was run by satanists. The trademark was said to be a satanic symbol being used as a result of a pact with the devil to ensure the company's success. A company executive had supposedly confessed the truth on *60 Minutes* or *Donahue*, depending on which version of the rumor you heard. By mid-1982 Proctor's consumer services department was getting 15,000 calls a month[12] from people asking about the company's connection with Satan. The company tried a counterpublicity campaign and both Donahue and a spokesman for *60 Minutes* publicly denied that such interviews existed, but the legend lived on. Ultimately, Proctor and Gamble was forced to change its trademark.

Another famous urban legend started in 1975. Suddenly there was a rash of reports by cattle ranchers in Colorado and nearby states of bizarre slaughter of cattle. Little meat had been eaten but the blood had been drained and the sexual organs and lips had been surgically removed. Speculation about the cause ranged from UFOs to satanic ritual to secret government experiments. A movie titled *Endangered Species* was rushed out to support the government experiment theory.

Expert animal pathologists were called in to investigate. They found that the deaths were nothing more than normal predator attacks and natural causes. The sex organs and lips had been removed, not with a knife, but by scavengers who took them because they were the softest and most accessible parts. The news reports had planted a belief in the minds of the ranchers that made them interpret normal deaths as confirmation of the rumors.

Eventually a few real cases appeared in Idaho and Montana. When police investigated they found it was the work of copycat satanic cultists who had read about the attacks in the newspapers and decided to try sacrificing cattle instead of the stray cats and dogs they usually used. This demonstrates another kind of positive feedback that keeps urban legends going: People read about the rumor and actually act it out, making it real. The idea of razor blades or poison in Halloween candy may have started as a rumor or a joke by one child, but it still has mothers checking candy decades later.[13]

The source of most urban legends usually remains forever a mystery, but the cattle mutilation was later revealed to be the result of an intentional hoax started as a joke by Dan Fry, the host of an astrology radio show called *Cosmic Age*. The joke got out of hand when the *Houston Post* published the story as a fact and then the wire services picked it up from them.

AN URBAN NIGHTMARE

Sexual abuse of small children by teachers in a preschool is one of the most horrible crimes imaginable. In August of 1983 a wave of revelations of such abuse spread like wildfire across California and other states. Many of the cases have now been dismissed, and some of the accused teachers are suing law enforcement officials for damages. The epidemic started in the McMartin preschool[14] in southern California when a mother, later diagnosed as a paranoid schizophrenic, called the police to report that her 2-year-old son had been sexually molested by one of the teachers. The police sent a letter to 200 McMartin parents to warn them of "possible criminal acts" such as "oral sex, fondling of genitals, buttocks or chest area, and sodomy."

By the beginning of November full-scale panic had spread among the parents. Over 350 children were interviewed by a consulting psychologist who used anatomically correct dolls and asked leading questions. Eventually the charges spread to include many other teachers and included charges that they jabbed scissors into a boy's eyes and even killed a baby and made the child drink its blood. The author of *Michelle Remembers*, a bizarre 1980 book based on a mental patient's repressed memories of satanic cults, was flown in as an expert. Charges continued to grow and now included babies being cooked and eaten, a child being put naked in a cage with a live lion, and making children perform in kiddie-porn movies.

The publicity from the McMartin case scared parents throughout the country and resulted in an epidemic of similar charges throughout the country.[15] Once the belief was planted in the minds of parents, police, and the "expert" psychologists, getting 3-year-olds to confirm them was easy. When an authority figure asks leading questions, children do their best to cooperate. Three-year-olds often have violent fantasies, particularly when they have had the trauma of being taken from their mother to be cared for by a stranger in a preschool. Even more importantly, interpretation of the children's answers is naturally distorted by perception to confirm the adult interviewer's beliefs.

After digging up the schoolyard for evidence with a backhoe, offering a $10,000 reward for the kiddie-porn movie, and staging the most expensive trial in California history, all of the McMartin defendants were acquitted. An investigation by the FBI Behavioral Research Unit concluded that "cross-contamination of ideas" between parent and law enforcement groups and between the children and the interrogators caused the fiasco. Positive feedback, acting on the fantasies of one crazed mother, grew uncontrollably into a nationwide epidemic.

BELIEF IN MAGIC

Why does it always seem to rain right after you have washed your car? Unless the world exists just on your behalf, this must be an illusion because *somebody* washes his car every day. The real difference is in our perception of the rainstorm, which changes after we have washed the car. A similar mental illusion happens after we have made a major decision such as getting married, getting divorced, or buying a new red car. It will suddenly seem that *everybody* is getting married, or divorced, or driving a red car. Your mind's natural tendency to look for unifying relationships actually changes your perception so that you notice things that confirm your decision. Disasters, such as airplane crashes, often seem to occur in threes. What really happens is that after a disaster, your mind is primed to notice other similar disasters. After the third one, the novelty wears off and you tire of making the connection.

Psychics benefit from our tendency to creatively distort our perception to fit our expectations. If you really believe in mystics and one says, "You have recently changed careers," you may be quite impressed that the psychic knew you were *thinking* of changing jobs. Even though the prediction was wrong, you can support your belief by stretching the interpretation a bit to make it right. If your friend asks you how the reading went you may reply, "Amazing, she knew that I was thinking about changing jobs." You would not even be aware that you distorted the fortune to fit your belief because it is simply the result of your mind's natural filling-in process.

Let me suggest a fascinating experiment for anyone who believes in psychics. Bring a small tape recorder to your next reading and secretly record the predictions. After a few days have passed, write down from memory a summary of the successful predictions. Then let a non-believer sit down with you and help you compare your recollections with the taped recording of what was actually said. Don't be surprised if there are some discrepancies. Memory distortions to confirm beliefs are amazingly convincing and require no dishonest intent. We want to have control and see order in the world so our mind simply obliges by helping us see reality according to our beliefs. Remember, anyone who can really see into the future should be living in a mansion: By simply choosing one winning lottery number or hot stock investment this prognosticator could be fixed for life.

AURAS AND ESP

Auras are a kind of colored halo effect around a person's head that is believed, by some people, to result from an energy flow. If you believe in auras, you will have no problem seeing them because your perception will fill in to match your belief. If you believe that nice people have green auras, your mind will fill in green or yellow based on your feelings about that person. It's really no different from filling in the blind spot in your vision. Scuba divers at great depths report seeing red fish even though there is no red light down there because it has been scattered and absorbed by the water above. Their mind simply fills in the red color because they know the fish is red from having seen it in shallow water.

If you believe in extrasensory perception, a call from a friend after you have thought about her is a confirmation of your powers. Such an experience feels truly amazing, but remember, the mind is very creative in finding patterns and connections; the mystical experiences that do click are the only ones we will notice and remember, while millions of other possible coincidences are ignored and forgotten. One coincidence is often enough to create a false belief, which will then be strengthened by the positive feedback of perception: Once you believe in your own or a friend's psychic powers, everything that you or the friend does is then experienced through perception in a way that confirms your belief. The psychic powers seem to grow with each experience until almost anything seems amazing. As a skeptic I once attended a demonstration by a world-famous psychic and was amazed, not by his powers, but by the way the believers in the crowd were so easily amazed. The most obvious generalizations based on people's visual appearance and manner were perceived as convincing proof of his powers. One sloppily dressed housewife in the audience was amazed and embarrassed that his psychic powers revealed that she had left her house in a mess.

Astrology retains its popularity as a result of the same need to believe. The predictions are written ambiguously so that they stimulate your imagination to make connections just like a Rorschach test. Since they predict several things every day, with selective forgetting of the predictions that don't come true, and creative distortion of the meanings, you are bound to be occasionally amazed. A 1984 Gallup Poll of teenagers found that 55% believed in astrology, considerably up from the 40% who believed in 1971. If you find the astrology predictions amazing, let me suggest an experiment: Try picking another sign for a month and reading those predictions as your own. You will find that the most astonishing thing of all is your own mind's ability to distort perception and memory to confirm your beliefs.

In designing control systems, engineers avoid positive feedback because of the instability it causes. When it is an inherent part of the system, as it is with the mind, negative feedback often needs to be added to stabilize the system. In your own mind that means learning to understand the creative distortions of your perception and memory and offsetting them with the negative feedback of common sense. Knowing that false beliefs can appear to be convincingly confirmed, we must continually challenge our own beliefs and try to look carefully at other viewpoints.

If you want to put this insight to work in your life, try making a list right now of beliefs you hold that seem to be opposed by people who may have started out in an opposite position. Think carefully about whether the confirming experiences that strengthened your belief could have been distorted by your perception. Try putting yourself in the position of someone with an opposing view and reexamining those experiences. Can you see them from the other viewpoint? Maybe you should reevaluate the belief. Try to form a habit of adding this negative feedback to your thinking habits to offset the positive feedback built into your consciousness.

Since your beliefs determine the nature of your reality, it is always wise to err on the positive side in your beliefs. If you believe that the world is a horrible place, it will surely seem to be so. If, on the other hand, you believe in goodness, you may be wrong, but the world will still *seem* better. In this sense you *can* create your own reality.

CHAPTER SEVEN

Hypnosis and Other Altered States

*There is nothing more difficult than to become critically aware
of the presuppositions of one's own thoughts. . . . Every
thought can be scrutinized directly except the thought by which
we scrutinize.*
—— *E. F. Schumacher, 1977*

Our own reality seems so inherent and secure that it is difficult to imagine just how different it can be if a few of the assumptions of our self-concept are changed. In many parts of Africa and in Pentecostal churches in Brazil, Haiti, Mexico, and even the United States, you will see parishioners seized by spirits, speaking in tongues (unknown languages), and otherwise demonstrating forms of consciousness that are frighteningly different from what we consider normal. Howling, spasms, and speaking in unknown languages are the norm during these church services. These altered states are not a physical ailment but simply a result of people *believing that they exist*. The exact form these altered states take varies from region to region because the concept varies. In the United States it has been estimated that there are some five million people who speak in tongues. Televangelists Oral Roberts, Jim Baker, Jimmy Swaggart, and Pat Robertson all speak in tongues but they avoid doing it on TV because they have found that it scares the uninitiated.[1]

In our culture people are expected to have a single well-defined self that is in charge at all times. When people depart from this model, many psychiatrists would regard it to be a mental problem called dissociative disorder, or dissociation. In other parts of the world, however, they have a different concept of what is normal. A 1972 cross-cultural study of some 400 non-Western societies by E. Bourguignon of Ohio State University found that 89% of them had "some institutionalized form of dissociation."

As any reading of ancient Greek mythology shows, it was once considered normal to hear voices of gods telling you what to do. Our modern concept of a singular self that is always in charge may in fact be only about 5000 years old. Most of us can be easily put into a state of hypnosis where we will follow the instructions of the hypnotist yet retain a "hidden observer" to observe and remember our actions. This is certainly a different model of consciousness than the one we call normal.

HYPNOTISM: BELIEVED-IN IMAGININGS

Hypnosis is another altered state that requires only belief to enter it. The way people act under hypnosis has changed through the years and still varies in different parts of the world. The hypnotic state is simply a different concept of consciousness where the mind fulfills different expectations. In the late 18th century Anton Mesmer used magnetic particles to put people in a hypnotic state that included violent fits and seizures. Other early hypnotists put subjects into a state resembling deep sleep. Experiments have shown that the characteristics of hypnosis will change significantly based on information given to the subject *before* any attempt is made to hypnotize them. The hypnotized subject seems to substitute an alternate self-concept based on their beliefs about the nature of the hypnotic state. An important part of this concept is that initiative and self-planning are suspended and control comes instead from the hypnotist.

Most people can be hypnotized if the basic requirements of *prestige* and *faith* are satisfied: The hypnotist must be in a position of *prestige*, and the subject must have *faith* in the hypnotist's ability. Hypnotizing intimate friends is difficult, but a famous stage hypnotist who has just demonstrated his powers has a very good chance of succeeding with almost any nonskeptic in the audience.

In the hypnotized state the subject loses initiative and lacks the desire to make and carry out plans of his own. Control is instead turned over to the hypnotist. This tendency to switch to a remote-control state may have an evolutionary basis. The herd instinct allowed evolving humans to blindly follow a leader in war or hunting situations. It is still seen in the mob mentality at riots, rock concerts, and lynchings. Just as all ducks in a formation follow the lead duck when flying, evolving humans had a survival advantage when they were sometimes able to blindly follow a leader. Normal reality testing is also suspended in the hypnotic state so that illogical illusions and distortions of reality are readily accepted. No special trance-inducing procedure is necessary if the basic prestige and faith requirements are met.

At religious revival meetings church members see visions of angels and other manifestations simply because their charismatic leader suggests it. A faith healer achieves the same kind of control as a hypnotist by simply touching the person to be healed. New age healing by transferring bioenergy uses visualization of an imaginary energy field and suggestion to effect (placebo) cures. Subjects report that they can feel the warmth of the bioenergy field suggested by the healer. The prestige and faith relationship works nicely in these situations without any specific hypnotic procedure.

Many altered states of consciousness are equivalent to self-hypnosis in that they are self-induced. Witch doctors and psychics put themselves into a state that alters consciousness by essentially switching to an alternate self-concept. In *channeling*, the psychic's consciousness is supposedly taken over by a departed spirit. As with hypnosis, belief in this state causes a believed-in imagining to be created that may seem real to the psychic. Unfortunately the messages produced are nothing more than confabulations.

Millions of believers in dianetics[2] have undergone a kind of therapy called auditing in which the therapist leads them back in time to when they were in the womb. The subject recalls traumatic experiences starting a few weeks after conception. Eventually almost every patient experiences a "sperm dream" that recovers the experiences of the sperm swimming up the channel to find the egg. Since no brain existed to do any remembering at that time, it is clear that the "memories" must be nothing but imaginative fantasies. In fact, the brain is not ready to store real verbalizable memories until almost the age of three.

Suggestion can sometimes affect body responses that are not consciously controllable by the average person. A hypnotist can suggest that the room is very hot and beads of sweat have been known to form on the forehead of some subjects. Suggestion seems to be able to work directly on modules that cannot usually be controlled by the self. People yawning in a crowd can make you yawn also. This is the result of suggestion even though most people cannot consciously initiate a real yawn. The placebo effect also demonstrates the power of suggestion over processes not under conscious control. Studies have shown that the immune system can be energized by suggestion or the placebo effect enough that it significantly changes the outcome of real diseases, including cancer.

Hypnotic suggestions of paralysis of limbs, blindness to certain objects, amnesia, insensitivity to pain, and even deafness demonstrate the power of the mind to distort our perception and abilities. Experiments have shown that *hypnotic subjects are actually in control of their own behavior but they convince themselves that the behavior is involuntary to fulfill their belief that they are hypnotized.* This is not a conscious deception any more than the one that we all do when we fail to see the blind spot in our field of vision. It is simply another demonstration of how strongly basic beliefs can affect the experience of consciousness. When people believe that they are deeply hypnotizable, their behavior and their conscious experience will confirm that belief.

When experimenters change the expectations of hypnosis by changing their comments and explanations before they begin,[3] they can totally change the outcome. For example, if subjects are told that the ability to *resist* suggestion is one indication of very deep hypnosis, they will successfully resist having their arm raise during a suggested visualization of an upward pull on their arm. If they are told that resistance is impossible under deep hypnosis, they will find that they are unable to stop their arm from raising.[4]

In one study subjects were asked to write a short essay about what happens in hypnosis before they were hypnotized. When hypnotized later, one of the subjects couldn't perform hypnotic tasks while standing. Checking her essay, they found that she had written, "The subject has to be reclining or sitting." Another kept waking from the trance whenever she was given a task where she had to see. She had written, "A person's eyes must be closed in order to be in a hypnotic trance." Another subject couldn't be hypnotized till the second attempt. His paper said, "Most people cannot be hypnotised the first time."[5]

Another confirmation of the role-enactment interpretation of hypnosis is that when hypnotized subjects are left with effects, such as a paralyzed arm, suggested earlier in the session uncanceled at the end of a hypnotic session, they will cancel it themselves[6] when they feel that the session is over. As soon as the subject thinks that the expectations have changed, the arm returns to normal operation. With posthypnotic suggestions, on the other hand, there is a clear expectation that certain behavior will occur on signal after the trance is over. Generally, the hypnotized subject always tries to act out his understanding of what the hypnotist expects.

CREATING HIDDEN OBSERVERS

Nicholas Spanos and a team of researchers at Carleton University in Ottawa, Canada, demonstrated the role-playing interpretation of hypnosis with the following experiment on hypnotically induced amnesia: They had eight highly hypnotizable students memorize a list of words and then suggested that they would forget of all the words until a prearranged signal. Three times the subjects were asked to remember the words. Each time they were beseeched to be completely honest in the interest of the scientific experiment and to try their best to remember the words. None of the students could breach the suggested amnesia until the prearranged signal released them from the suggested amnesia.

The experiment was repeated but this time the students were told that they would have a hidden observer in their head that could be accessed whenever their shoulder was touched and that this hidden observer would remember everything. All of the subjects remembered the words while their shoulder was touched but forgot them otherwise.

In another variation of the experiment the subjects were given two hidden observers: Touching the right shoulder would allow remembering abstract words while touching the left would allow concrete words to be remembered. Otherwise all words were forgotten until the prearranged signal. Again all of the subjects performed exactly according to the instructions. When the subjects were interviewed after the experiment they all described the experience as beyond their voluntary control—as though their consciousness and memories changed depending upon which shoulder was touched. This ability to redefine consciousness with hypnotic suggestion demonstrates clearly how profoundly our conscious experience is defined by our beliefs.

A suggestion that a potato is an apple makes it possible for the subject to happily eat a raw potato and think it delicious. A bottle of ammonia can be made to smell like wonderful perfume. If a hypnotist places five postage stamps on a white card and then points at two of the stamps and suggests that they are not there, the subject will insist that there are only three stamps, pointing at each of the three stamps he sees as he counts them. If the stamps are scrambled, he will still count only the same three stamps[7] in their new positions, denying the existence of the two tabooed stamps. *In order to find the three allowed stamps the forbidden stamps must have been seen at some unconscious level to know enough to ignore them.* This filtering of consciousness to fit beliefs is simply the way the brain works.

Under hypnosis you can be made to think you are Napoleon Bonaparte and you will try to react as you think he would. If the hypnotist suggests that you regress to being a child of a certain age, you will imagine that to be true, talk baby talk, write in a childish scrawl, and even answer questions about yourself at that age. You can even be progressed into the future and you will play the role of yourself at age 80.

Past life regression[8] under hypnosis was the subject of a study by researchers at Carleton University. Under hypnosis and suggestion of regression to a past life, 35 out of 110 college students tested recalled a past life identity. During the hypnotic regression they were questioned about the times, their name, and particularly about commonly known facts such as currency, the name of the ruler of their country, and whether their country was at war. The past lives reported were found to be generally limited to times and places familiar to the students. The facts given usually failed to agree with the verifiable facts of the imagined time and place. The researchers concluded that "past-life reports are fantasies that subjects construct on the basis of their often limited and inaccurate historical information."

Posthypnotic suggestions can make the subject do bizarre things after they are out of the hypnotic state, for example, crawling on the floor in response to a specific signal from the hypnotist. When this is done the subject usually rationalizes the behavior by saying something like, "This is an interesting floor." We are clearly in the habit of confidently rationalizing behavior even when we have no idea what caused it.

CREATING MULTIPLE CONSCIOUSNESS

Hypnosis can be used to alter consciousness in ways that split the mind[9] into multiple entities. E. Hilgard of Stanford University performed numerous experiments in which he used hypnosis to set up a hidden observer in the subject that communicated only through *automatic writing*. In one such experiment he suggested a numbing of one hand to consciousness but not to the hidden observer. He could then dip the subject's numbed hand into ice water and the subject would claim to feel nothing though the hidden observer would simultaneously write down a message indicating pain. When the subjects were interviewed after the experiment, one said he was annoyed at the superior attitude of the hidden observer, which seemed amused at his self-deception. Another subject said it was comforting to have a "guardian angel" there to protect his body from his own failure to recognize the pain.

When a hypnotist creates these bizarre alterations of consciousness the result is almost like what would happen in an actor's workshop except that the subject truly believes the role he is acting out. Good method actors in fact do just that: They must truly believe the role they are playing. Good hypnotic subjects may really just be good actors.

Automatic writing without hypnosis used to be a popular way to tap into unconscious thoughts. Gertrude Stein used automatic writing in all of her later books. The Ouija board uses the same principle, with unconscious forces on the hands moving a pointer touched lightly with the fingertips to spell out answers. All that is required is belief. Consciousness can take many forms since it is defined by our beliefs. People who keep daily journals develop a kind of observer module that has a life of its own.

Facilitated Communications[10] (FC) is a technique, originated in Australia in the 1980s, that provided hope for millions of parents of autistic children. Since the autistic child cannot communicate, FC gave them a voice by having a "facilitator," usually a special education teacher, support one hand of the autistic child and help the child to type out messages on a keyboard. The facilitator sensed where the hand wanted to go and simply helped the child to type his own reply. Wonderful results were obtained, with children who had previously seemed to have extremely low IQs doing well in advanced subjects.

Though the movement still has many advocates, the unfortunate fact seems to be that FC is just an illusion.

Dedicated facilitators with honest intentions seem to be actually unconsciously using the child's hand as a Ouija board to write messages from their own mind. In controlled experiments it has been found that FC works only when the facilitator knows the answer and can see the keyboard. The training courses for facilitators apparently created a split consciousness much like Hilgard produced in his hypnotic subjects. Though the facilitators are not conscious of it, a separate module in their own brain is providing the answers for the children. In 1995 the FC movement is still very much alive; in fact, a facilitated book supposedly written by an autistic child was just released. This is another example of the sometimes tragic mistakes caused by our misunderstanding of the nature of consciousness.

CHAPTER EIGHT

Psychotherapy and Multiple Personalities

Where id was, there ego shall be.
—— *Sigmund Freud, 1930*

The man who once cursed his fate, now curses himself—and pays his psychoanalyst.
—— *John W. Gardner, 1968*

A mental illness called *hysteria* was extremely common among women in Freud's time. Hysteria could cause paralysis, loss of consciousness, seizures, blindness, and other symptoms of physical illness. Hysteric patients were found to be mostly women who were very easily hypnotized and also needful of more attention and respect from others. Hysteria is rare today, but people with this profile now suffer from other syndromes that were rare in Freud's day. Multiple personality disorder (MPD)[1] is one amazing example.

Though it was previously considered quite rare, in the past decade over 20,000 people [2] have been diagnosed as having MPD. One of the catalysts for this explosion was probably the best-selling fictionalized book *Sybil*,[3] which was published in 1973 and sold over four million copies. An earlier book and movie *The Three Faces of Eve* also helped define and popularize the idea of multiple personalities.

Once MPD had been defined in the popular imagination, positive feedback soon transformed it into an epidemic. A few psychiatrists started specializing in the disorder and collecting patients together into group therapy sessions where they could reinforce each other. A special technical journal was created, books were written, and conventions and workshops were organized. Before long MPD became a popular alternative for the same kind of easily hypnotized, frustrated, and powerless people who had previously chosen hysteria as an attention-getting alternative to normal behavior.

Using hypnosis to find and name alter personalities, MPD therapists find an average of 7 personalities, but as many as 50 have been reported. After much practice it becomes possible to talk to any of the personalities by name—just like switching channels on a TV set. The problem is that *the personalities may have nothing to do with real modules of the mind*.[4] The hypnotized subject uses all of her creativity to try to meet the expectations of the hypnotist. Sometimes the alter personalities write with different handwriting and speak in different voices. This is very imaginative, but what could be the basis other than fantasy? Clearly different modules share the same speech and writing structures in the brain. Hypnotized subjects suspend their own reality testing and create the whole character complete with a distinctive voice—just as an actor would. Under hypnosis, creating a new alter personality is no harder than regressing to a past life or acting out your own imagined future.

LOBSTERS AND UNICORNS

The therapist–patient relationship has the perfect *prestige and faith* ingredients to make it possible for patients to enter the receptive state without any specific hypnotic procedure. In this state the patient unconsciously suspends normal reality testing and becomes dedicated to satisfying the expectations of the therapist.

Alter personalities, or alters, discovered in therapy tend to have characteristics that vary greatly depending on the particular therapist's expectations. One therapist reported in the professional journal *Dissociation* that he encountered "demons, angels, sages, lobsters, chickens, tigers, a unicorn, and God" in his search for alter personalities. "The inscapes in which they exist," he wrote, "have ranged from labyrinthine tunnels and mazes to castles in enchanted forests, high-rise office buildings, and even a separate galaxy."[5] More often alters are the kind of stereotyped characters one would expect to come out of a drama improvisation workshop.

The number of alters tends to grow as therapy continues because many therapists are continually trying to discover more. Just how suggestive these techniques can be is shown by the following quote from an article on therapy techniques[6] written by the director of a hospital MPD program:

> I also try to recruit other alters to the therapy by asking if any other parts of the mind that I have not yet met would like to contribute their thoughts or share any concerns or opinions. If there is no response, I may say, "Since there is no answer, may I assume that those of you I have not met are in agreement?" This often leads to inner speech or emergence by other alters . . .

Once a patient has a firmly established multiple personality, the symptoms can become so bizarre that it seems amazing they could have gone unnoticed during 7 years of therapy. Yet the average duration of psychotherapy before MPD is diagnosed is 6.9 years.[7]

Another disturbing fact is that some leading MPD specialists find that a high percentage of their patients end up firmly convinced that they have been victims of satanic cults that practice human sacrifice and cannibalism. This seemingly unrelated finding is another frightening demonstration of what happens when the imaginative role-playing of hypnosis is misinterpreted as something real and is reinforced by positive feedback.

When I originally began researching the MPD literature I had hoped that it would provide insight on the modules of the normal mind. What I found instead was a bizarre demonstration of how false beliefs can flourish, hypnosis can be misunderstood, and the awesome power of suggestion can totally restructure a person's self-concept and consciousness. The emotional pain many of these patients go through is ample proof of the benefit of having some degree of unity in your self-concept.

Understanding the true multiplicity of the mind can enhance your understanding of your own and other people's behavior. However, letting your imagination run wild and create an unruly collection of stereotyped characters, devils, and animals can only lead you further away from self-understanding and perhaps even into madness.

Somewhere buried in the 20,000 recent cases of MPD are undoubtedly some real cases where the spontaneous organization process actually produced a unique brain organization with two self modules. In one case reported in 1955[8] a 20-year-old woman who was normally "dependent, shy, self-effacing, affectionate, and obedient" would sometimes switch to an almost opposite personality that was "impulsive, irresponsible, mischievous, and vindictive." In this case there was clear evidence that the mechanism for activating one or the other half of the brain was faulty. When the shy personality was active she was always numb on the left side of her body and hypersensitive on the right. When the vindictive personality was active this pattern reversed itself.

Another pair of cases reported in 1993[9] both had temporal lobe epilepsy. By injecting a sedative in the artery in either side of the neck the doctors were able to disable one side of the patient's brain or the other. In both cases the two personalities seemed to have formed in opposite sides of the patient's brain. In these authentic cases the epilepsy and the faulty orientation mechanism provided a physical mechanism for creating the separation of memories necessary for true split personalities. In normal people, separate modules all receive the same sensory inputs but may interpret the memories differently because of their different specialized viewpoints.

FINDING YOUR MODULES

The idea of using therapy to improve the relationship between the modules of your mind is a fascinating and promising one. The problem is that *you must first correctly identify the modules.* People generally have no awareness of the other modules of their mind so that patients under hypnosis simply confabulate to satisfy the therapist. Once these imaginary personalities are identified and named, they take on a life of their own. The patient's self-concept begins to include the separate named entities, which were originally just confabulations. Efforts to integrate imaginary entities simply build fantasy on a foundation of fantasy.

The real modules of your mind are not easy to identify, but the fact that they must evolve from simple beginnings, usually in childhood, is an important reality check. Identifying your modules requires hard detective work, observation, and an understanding of evolutionary principles. The modules compete with each other to control behavior, and only the fittest survive. Part of this evolutionary process is the way a module relates to other modules.

If your self module shuts down completely when you engage in sports, art, or other flow activities, it is because those activities are more successful without any second-guessing from the self. The fact that this leaves a gap in your conscious memory is normally not a problem, so the habit becomes firmly ingrained. People who keep their self module alert in such situations will never be great athletes or artists. In fact, *concentration is often just another word for dissociation.* Of course there are times when concentration can cause you to miss appointments, forget to watch after children, or even burn the house down with a cooking fire. The ideal is to develop the teamwork of your mental modules for maximum effectiveness—and that requires some, but not too much, dissociation.

We all have multiple personalities in a manner of speaking, but people differ in how well their modules work together as an integrated team. Certainly some people have problems caused by poorly integrated dissociated personalities where one module doesn't know what the other is doing. A common experience of dissociation is when you are absorbed in a flow activity, like driving, reading, or art, and you find that you have a gap in your memory. This simply means that your self module was not paying attention and therefore remembers nothing. This is usually not a problem, but if you have no memory of a shopping spree, a drinking binge, or other destructive behavior it can cause serious problems.

Many children have imaginary playmates that develop unique personalities. Children often talk to these playmates by name and even answer in a different voice. Likewise, many normal adults talk to themselves when alone. In fact, normal variations in people include varying degrees of dissociation between modules. When a questionnaire normally used to screen mental patients for MPD was given to 415 students[10] in a wide range of majors at the University of Idaho, 8.9% of them scored above the threshold that usually indicates MPD or other dissociative disorders. Clearly many normally functioning people have dissociative experiences.

Usually, a module that is not in control is still in the receptive mode, following and remembering what is happening. However, each module has its own mental habits. Since *the self module is the one that fills out questionnaires*, high dissociative scores could indicate that the self module is in the habit of not being receptive at certain times. In some cases this can be a good mental habit indicating that the self module is standing back completely to avoid interfering in areas where it is not qualified.

PSYCHOTHERAPY AND REALITY

Many of the famous names in psychology have observed the fact that the mind is clearly split into separate and sometimes conflicting entities. Freud, for example, called them the ego, the id, and the superego. His ego corresponds roughly to the self module. Carl Jung listed a much wider cast of characters. In addition to the ego, he also included the persona, the shadow, the anima, the wise man, the self, and many others. Eric Berne, a leader in transactional analysis, identified three major "ego states," which he called the parent, the adult, and the child.

All of these methods of dividing up the mind made sense to their creators and continue to make sense for their disciples who use them in the practice of psychotherapy. Their original appeal may be partly dependent on how closely they match the actual organization of the therapist's mind. However, once you believe in any of these theories, positive feedback will guarantee that the belief will be convincingly confirmed many times a day.

The problem is that for a scientific method of treatment to be effective, the original assumptions that form its basis must be true. While it is useful to view the mind as made up of independent modules, it is important that you get the nature of the division right. The hundreds of conflicting schools of psychology depend far too much on authoritative principles laid down by their founders and too little on sound scientific principles. The principles of self-organization and Darwinian evolution provide just such a sound basis.

The multi-billion-dollar therapy industry is currently at a stage similar to 19th century medicine when doctors bled their patients and often did them more harm than good. Numerous studies have tried to measure the effectiveness of psychotherapy and have come up with embarrassing results. For example, a 1977 metaanalysis by Smith and Glass[11] published in *American Psychologist*, which compared results of nearly 400 psychotherapy outcome studies, concluded, "Despite volumes devoted to theoretical differences among different schools of psychotherapy, the results of research demonstrate negligible differences in the effects produced by different therapy types."

Though that study found therapy to be helpful for most people treated, it had two important flaws: (1) It included some behavioral therapy studies, and (2) it ignored the placebo effect. In 1983, Prioleau, Murdock, and Brody of Wesleyan University did another analysis that included only studies of real patients under nonbehavioral psychotherapy where a placebo treatment[12] was offered. The placebos varied from sugar pills with weekly visits where the discussion was limited to the pill itself to group therapy sessions where the leader purposely kept the discussion on unrelated subjects. They found no difference between the effectiveness of the placebo treatments and the professional psychotherapy! Since some therapists are clearly better than others, this null result implies that there must be some therapists who consistently make their patients worse to cancel the results of the good therapists. In their summary, the researchers said, "after about 500 outcome studies have been reviewed—we are still not aware of a single convincing demonstration that the benefits of psychotherapy exceed those of placebos for real patients." If psychotherapy was a drug it would be banned by the FDA because it fails to meet their requirement that effective treatments must be more effective than placebos.

TREATING THE OFFENDING MODULES

The problem with any talk therapy is that the patient's self module does the talking about behavior that is often controlled by other modules about which the self module has no direct knowledge. The result then may be *an improvement in the self module's ability to explain and understand the behavior but no change in the actual behavior*. A side benefit of this improved understanding may be an improved ability for the self module to seize control when it recognizes the behavior. The real goal, however, should be changing the behavior itself, and this requires retraining the errant module itself by doing corrective work *when it is actually in control*. To teach someone to dance you must get his dance module involved with actual movement and visual demonstrations. If you simply talk about the principles of a dance you will develop a verbal understanding but no ability to dance. For therapy to be really effective it must be directed at the modules that are producing the errant behavior. Some in-context behavior modification actually does this and has proven amazingly effective.

For example, phobic disorders such as agoraphobia and panic attacks are very effectively treated by application of *in vivo* (real life) exposure to the sources of fear for prolonged periods in gradually increasing difficulty. The result is a gradual decrease in the fear via a process called habituation. For example, for an agoraphobic patient who is afraid to leave her house, the therapist makes a house call and helps her overcome the fear in small steps. The first step would be to simply stand in the doorway together until the panic passes. The next step would be standing on the front porch, and then on the sidewalk, and so forth until eventually the patient has regained complete freedom of movement. Homework assignments between therapist visits help the patients learn to progress on their own. The cognitive part of the treatment involves teaching the patient techniques for distracting their mind from negative thoughts and also learning to interpret the feelings of panic in a healthier way. The principle is to "feel the fear and do it anyway." Cure rates as high as 80%[13] have been reported with very few relapses. A similar technique is very effective for obsessive-compulsive ritualistic behavior. The important thing is to do the work in the same real-life situations that would normally trigger the behavior so that the module with the problem will be engaged.

TRAINING YOUR FIGHT MODULE

Many marital and relationship problems are a result of an inability to settle differences without ugly fights. If a couple has problems when their fight modules engage, it helps very little for each person to go to a separate psychiatrist and let their self module spend endless hours discussing its self-serving rationalizations about what happened. Since the self module was only *observing* the fights anyway, the discussion is academic—almost like sending a friend who witnessed the fights to discuss them for you.

As any skilled debater can tell you, arguing can be a pleasant and satisfying experience when both parties observe certain rules. The problem with ugly fights is that they are explosions of tension that has built up from exercising self-control to avoid settling differences because of previous bad experiences with your fight module.

Often, bad patterns are learned from parents who didn't know how to fight constructively. A good therapist or a friend can act as a referee while you and your partner discuss topics that have caused fights in the past. This way the actual behavior of your fight module can be modified while it is engaged. Ideally you should start with the easiest issues that will actually engage the fight module and work up to more difficult issues as you gain confidence in your improved skills.

The referee should be neutral and focus only on the argument techniques being used. One technique that must be totally forbidden is the *personal attack*: Discussions should be about issues and actions, not about insulting generalizations about the opponent. In other words, "You did" is allowed, but "you are . . . " isn't. Having a referee to monitor the discussion and point out violations to this rule can eventually train the fight module to monitor itself and change this destructive behavior pattern. Another important rule is to *listen* to what the opponent has to say. Again the referee provides corrective feedback whenever this rule is broken to correct the bad habits and keep the discussion constructive.

Once the two fight modules have experienced the satisfaction of a good, constructive fight, they gain the confidence that they can settle differences without things turning ugly. Though the self module is not in control, it is watching and gaining confidence that it can safely let the argument happen. Differences can then be settled by the fight modules themselves *before* frustration builds to a breaking point.

Other psychological problems can also benefit from doing work while the correct module is in control. Psychodrama and role-playing exercises can engage the proper module and then try to modify behavior and develop better skills. A salesperson develops a sales module that can be engaged during realistic role playing exercises to provide improvements that would be impossible to achieve by reading books or listening to lectures. A boss with an unpleasant boss module can develop his or her skills by role playing with someone trained in personal skills.

Problems with intimacy and sex are best worked on with a lover who engages a cuddling module and constructively reinforces good behavior. Just as the behavioral treatment for phobic behaviors gradually tackles more and more fearful situations, the treatment should start with easy situations and gradually build confidence while attacking more and more challenging situations. A common cause of sex and intimacy problems is an abrupt switching to another inappropriate module that defensively takes control. Building the confidence of the cuddling module helps it keep control. Often the offender is the self module, which is afraid to lose control because it doesn't trust the cuddling module.

There are some problems that do respond well to talk therapy. Any problem that is primarily a result of bad patterns of thinking of the self module itself are candidates. Certain kinds of depression, for example, are effectively treated by cognitive therapy. The therapist works with the patient to identify the faulty thought patterns causing the depression and helps him practice looking at problems in healthier ways.

Often neurosis is not a disease at all but simply the result of unrealistic expectations about life. Our media creates a false belief that life is easy, which causes some people to have a very low tolerance for mental pain. Just as people's response to physical pain can vary greatly with learned beliefs, mental pain can be the result of bad mental habits magnifying insignificant misfortunes. The truth is that it takes a lot of work just to keep food on the table, people die, cars break down, and bosses, parents, and mates aren't perfect. Many depressed people simply need to face up to the fact that "shit happens" and learn to face real life bravely, enjoying the good times and paying the dues as cheerfully as possible.

One of the problems with the idea of directing treatment at the proper module is that it is sometimes difficult to even identify the modules. Though most people have a fight module, a cuddling module, a childish play module, a school/work module, and a driving the car module, the unique life and brain organization of each individual makes further generalization difficult. It is therefore very important to first get to know your module structure. It would be nice if hypnosis could access this, as some MPD specialists seem to think it can, but unfortunately the only answer is careful observation and detective work. Your life history, siblings, friends, teachers, jobs, children, and a thousand influences mold your module structure. The exact timing and sequence of these influences can make a profound difference, because modules tend to evolve in a complex interaction with your previous developmental history. In the next chapter we will look further at how you can identify your own unique module structure.

PSYCHIATRY AND FALSE BELIEFS

In most fields false beliefs are quickly disproved by reality and die a natural death. If an engineer has a faulty idea for a new invention, the reality of a prototype that works or doesn't work will quickly eliminate the bad ideas. In the mental health field the opposite is true: The placebo effect and the positive feedback of subjective measures of success often make even bad ideas seem to work. This problem is exacerbated by the long-standing tradition in medicine of considering it unethical to criticize another doctor's treatments.

In the 1940s and 1950s tens of thousands of frontal lobotomies[14] were performed on hapless mental patients. In this operation the entire frontal lobe of the patient's brain was destroyed using an instrument like an ice pick. Dr. Egas Moniz, the inventor of this grotesque operation, won the 1949 Nobel Prize in Medicine for its invention. During the frontal lobotomy's heyday, the mainstream of psychiatry was uncritically enthusiastic about the operation. After initial relief, many of the patients eventually exhibited worse behavior, while others degenerated into a vegetable like state. The patients themselves were unaware that they were now essentially zombies because they could still talk and fill gaps as needed to construct a conscious reality based on what was left of their brain. During the first ten years of the lobotomy craze very little was published against it, again because of the long-standing taboo against publicly criticizing another physician's treatment.

A modern-day nightmare of even greater proportions is the memory recovery movement. Sigmund Freud may have set the stage for this one when he invented the idea of the Oedipus and Electra complexes. The Electra complex is Freud's idea that every little girl has fantasies of having sexual intercourse with her father. Armed with this concept, many therapists dismissed their female patients' true memories of childhood sex abuse as nothing more than the standard Electra fantasies. In reality, childhood sex abuse has been found to be much more common than previously acknowledged. A random survey of 930 women in 1978[15] found that 12% said they had experienced unwanted actual or attempted incest by the age of 14.

The justifiable anger at this situation prompted an uprising of indignation that grew into the memory recovery movement. It is the perfect archetype for the plight of women in our society: Fathers rape their daughters, and then male psychiatrists dismiss their memories as fantasies. In the 1980s an informal network of feminist therapists in the Boston area began using hypnotic age regression and dream analysis to reawaken repressed memories of incest in their patients. In 1988, a book by Ellen Bass and Laura Davis called *The Courage to Heal* made the repressed memory search a national phenomenon. It has since sold over 750,000 copies.

The book begins with a long list of the symptoms of childhood sexual abuse that everybody essentially exhibits. The list includes many almost universal feelings like *feeling powerless, feeling different from other people, having trouble expressing your feelings, being prone to depression, feeling alienated and lonely, clinging to people you care about*, and *having trouble feeling motivated*. If you have any of these symptoms, the book claims, you are probably an incest victim and need to begin working to recover your lost memories. Support groups have been formed throughout the country where people who haven't yet recovered their own memories of incest can listen to the recovered memories of fellow victims to help them find their own hidden memories.

Therapists who specialize in memory work often use hypnosis, dream analysis, make-believe visualizations, and other suggestive techniques to bring out the repressed memories. Even without hypnosis, the information recalled in psychotherapy is always profoundly affected by the beliefs of the therapist. As Carol Tavris said,[16]

> people in psychoanalysis have Freudian dreams, people in Jungian therapy have archetypal dreams, people in primal scream therapy remember being born, and people in past-lives therapy remember being Julius Caesar (or whoever).

The use of hypnosis for memory recovery has been condemned by the Council on Scientific Affairs of the American Medical Association. Their 1985 report in the *Journal of the American Medical Association* stated that

> recollections obtained during hypnosis not only fail to be more accurate but actually appear to be generally less reliable than recall. . . . Consequently, hypnosis may increase the appearance of certitude without a concurrent increase of veracity.

In spite of this clear statement, a 1992 survey of 860 therapists[17] attending national conventions found that *84% thought that hypnotic age regression was a useful technique and 75% believed that hypnosis enables people to accurately remember forgotten events.* The average respondent had education above a master's degree and had been in clinical practice for more than 11 years.

Memory is *not* like a videotape recorder that records everything you see. The bits and pieces that are really remembered fade with time just as those dates you memorized in sixth grade history class have faded. With effort we can sometimes recall some of them, but hypnotic age regression, dream analysis, and other extreme measures will never bring most of them back. The chemical changes in the brain that originally recorded memories can simply fade away forever. Trying too hard to recover memories simply forces the mind to fill in with imagination.

The unfortunate fact is that once a memory has been "recovered" it becomes convincingly real in the mind of the victim, and there is no way to test it for reality and no way to remove it. After much rehearsal and discussion it may become even more vivid than a real memory. There is no way to tell how many families have been tragically destroyed by the effects of battles over accusations based on false recovered memories.

Real memories that have been ignored or distorted by denial do require work to sort through and reinterpret, but they are not completely invisible. They lurk in the back of the mind in the same manner as our, usually denied, knowledge of our own mortality. Perhaps the worst thing about the recovered memory movement is that the backlash from their excesses may make it difficult for real victims of abuse trying to come out of denial to be believed.

SATANIC MEMORIES

Recovered memories are almost impossible to refute because the only other witness could be in denial. However, one certain indication that recovered memories are often false is the fact that about *18% of the victims who recover memories of childhood sexual abuse after a long period of unawareness also eventually recover memories of satanic abuse.*[18] In fact, some therapists report that half of their patients[19] are survivors of such abuse. In most recovered memories of ritual abuse the patient gets so carried away with the fantasy that their claims are clearly impossible.

A recent book by a survivor of ritual abuse includes a survey of 52 other survivors.[20] All had recovered memories of ritual abuse and were still in therapy at the time of the study. The results showed that 36% said they had been *"forced to breed children who were later sacrificed."* This means that, though friends or neighbors must have seen them go through the pregnancy, nobody got suspicious when the baby suddenly disappeared! The same survey found that 88% had witnessed or participated in human sacrifice, 82% with cannibalism.

The sheer number of unsolved murders this would represent doesn't tally with reality. Fifty percent of the respondents said the abuse took place *in their church*—usually in the basement—and 67% said their fathers perpetrated the abuse, while 42% named their mother. These runaway fantasies demonstrate the total instability that results from unchecked positive feedback.

Once again, a book is implicated for spreading the idea of satanic ritual abuse and stimulating imaginations all over the country. The book *Michelle Remembers*, published in 1980, was written by a psychiatrist and his patient. It recalls in detail satanic rituals Michelle now believes she was forced to attend with her mother when she was a child. These memories were recovered years later under a kind of self-hypnosis. Though the book didn't mention it, Michelle's two sisters have no memory of any abuse, and neighbors describe their mother as a "charming person." One person's confabulation under hypnosis thus becomes a kind of urban legend, spread through the media and victim groups to resurface in recovered memories all over the country.

A recent survey of American Psychological Association members[21] found that *over 12% indicated that they had treated one or more patients who recalled ritual abuse*. Many of the respondents told of treating dozens—and in some cases hundreds—of such victims. Clearly a sizable minority in the psychotherapy profession have a dangerously poor understanding of the nature of memory and of the ease with which they can lead their vulnerable believing clients into madness.

All memories are changeable. They can be created, elaborated, and modified after the fact. Our behavior patterns are based on the same neural mechanisms as memory, so changing behavior is essentially the same as changing memory. The job of the therapist should be to change our interpretation of memories and retrain our behavior in ways that will make us happier, more effective people. Our past can't be changed, but its effect on us can.

Unfortunately, many therapists use their patients to vent their own anger at parents or the opposite sex. In doing this they often do irreparable harm—often creating traumatic memories or changing pleasant memories into traumatic nightmares. Raging against parents who you formerly loved is not therapeutic because it modifies your memories in a negative direction. Learning to understand your parents' human weaknesses and love them anyway should be the goal of therapy. All parents try their best but fail in varying degrees because of human imperfection. The Norman Rockwell vision of the perfect family exists only in fantasy. We are bound to find life disappointing if we can't even learn to be tolerant of our own parents' shortcomings, as we all must live in a world of imperfect people.

CHAPTER NINE

The Infant Brain

> But what am I?
> An infant crying in the night:
> An infant crying for the light:
> And with no language but a cry.
> —— *Tennyson, 1850*

Months before a baby is born, all 10 billion neurons that will constitute its adult brain are already in place. Neurons cannot divide as other cells do, but an infant's brain still grows significantly in the first two years. Most of that growth results from further development of the rich network of interconnections (axons and dendrites) and surrounding tissue that supports and insulates the neurons (Figure 9).

Ultimately a neuron may have interconnections to as many as a quarter of a million other neurons; the average, however, is more like 10,000 connections. Though most of the interconnections look like the wild tangle of plants in a jungle, some sensory and motor connections are quite regular and clearly follow a genetically determined plan. Some of these interconnections seem to grow by a "survival of the fittest" process in which ineffective connections don't survive. This process works properly only if there is sensory stimulation during the critical growth period.

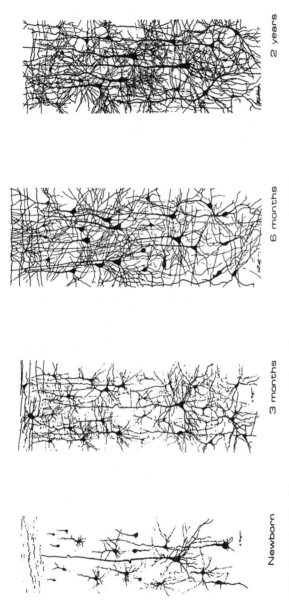

FIGURE 9. All of the neurons you will ever have are present months before birth, but the connecting dendrites and axons that join them continue to develop during the first two years of life. (From *Brain and Psyche* by Jonathan Winson, Doubleday, New York, 1985.)

For example, visual information is connected to the brain by at least 20 different genetically determined *maps*. These maps are areas of the brain where preprocessed visual information is connected according to a very specific wiring scheme. Each map handles an aspect of vision, such as movement and color, and different categories of shapes, such as lines of different angles. If these aspects of vision aren't exercised during the critical first two years of life they will never develop properly. When vision is repaired in an adult who has been blinded by an optical problem from birth, very little useful vision results even though the eye itself may function perfectly. Even after years of practice, full visual ability will never be achieved because of the fact that these nerve paths didn't grow in properly in the first place.

If a child with severe astigmatism[1] (bad focus on lines of a certain orientation) doesn't receive corrective lenses until after six years of age, there will be a permanent loss of sharpness for lines of that direction. The specialized, preprocessed connections that handle the blurred line orientation apparently don't develop properly during the critical period.

Studies have shown that babies who spend most of the first year of their life lying in their cribs develop abnormally slowly. Some of these infants couldn't sit up at 21 months of age, and less than 15% could walk by the age of three.[2] They would scream and try to avoid strangers or novel objects or toys and spend hours on end engaged in repetitive movements such as rocking and head banging in a quest for stimulation.[3]

Evolution always works by adding new structures on top of ancient ones inherited from lower animals. Many of the newer structures of the brain are incomplete at birth because the infant can survive at a basic level using the older structures inherited from earlier- and faster-developing ancestors. A human infant's cry follows the same rising and falling melodic pattern as the separation call of a monkey.[4] As this is refined into speech by later-developing higher parts of the brain, sentences continue to have the same melodic pattern, rising in pitch at the start and falling at the end.

The infant's progress in learning new behaviors and abilities is paced by this gradual completion of the wiring of the brain. At birth, speech would be impossible because that part of the baby's brain is still not fully developed. Memories that can be verbally recalled are not possible until the child is almost three because the connections between neurons are incomplete.

Since sucking on the mother's breast has been and is crucial to evolutionary survival, the neurons for these reflex responses in the older lower part of the brain are ready to go at birth. To use computer terminology, the growth of the interconnecting network between neurons shown in Figure 9 can be thought of as hardware development. When the neural hardware is ready, the infant's mental software can begin to develop. The software part of development relies, not on physical changes, but on a learning process. *Learning is achieved whenever a successful outcome causes the synapses of the specific neural connections in the brain that caused that outcome to be strengthened.* The synapses are tiny gaps at each connection point between the neurons that can control the efficacy of the connection. Scientists have recently found that the neuron actually sends a signal back to the active synapses whenever it fires.

This "back-propagating" action potential[5] may be the basis of learning and self-organization.

THE BEGINNINGS OF SPONTANEOUS ORGANIZATION

When the baby's mouth first finds the nipple and gets a milk reward, the synapses active during that behavior become strengthened, thus increasing the chances of success in the future. Clusters of neurons begin to organize spontaneously as soon as the baby is exposed to the external world. If the baby's hands knead the breast and get more milk, that refinement is added to the nursing module's behavior. As the baby grows beyond nursing age, this specialized module, as a result of tireless exploration, continues to develop. Virtually everything that can be put into the mouth is tried at least once. As the child grows to adulthood this module evolves and may continue to be active during smoking a pipe or cigarette, making love, or drinking. A child may seek comfort after stress by sucking his thumb, blanket, or pacifier. Smoking rituals often have an uncanny similarity. Watch an adult male in a bar after he has been rebuffed by a woman and you will almost surely see him immediately raise his glass to his lips—just like a pacifier.

Another basic behavior module of infancy is one that is engaged during crying. As the child grows, this module evolves into more sophisticated temper tantrums. Every adult has a behavior module that has evolved from this basic crying module. It takes control in certain emotional fighting situations. If parents try from the beginning to allow the child to express anger in a constructive way rather than forbid anger entirely they set the stage for development of a healthy fight module.

If you watch an infant's movements you can see an almost continual random experimentation. Occasionally something accidentally works, causing the synapses involved to be reinforced so that the behavior can be repeated. If you practice biofeedback or even try to wiggle your ears, you will find yourself doing the same kind of random experimentation. You don't know what you are doing but you just keep trying things until voila!—you see your ears wiggle in the mirror. If you practice it repeatedly you will find that it gets easier each time as the new pattern of synapses gradually gets refined and reinforced.

New modules spontaneously organize whenever the experience of existing modules gives them no advantage in reacting to a new situation. If a new cluster of neurons wins the competition for control, then it will be reinforced instead of an existing module. When the mother first looks into the baby's eyes and responds to the baby's eye movements, a new module may be created that can evolve into a whole repertoire of responsive behavior. Grasping an extended finger and finding a playful interaction can be the beginning of another module or simply a refinement of an existing one. Very subtle differences in circumstances can cause development to start down a different path, which can ultimately have a major impact.

This sensitivity to very small changes is one of the characteristics of self-organizing systems that have profound implications in child development. At certain critical points in the child's development a tiny difference in conditions can determine whether a new module is born or an old one is refined. As a result of many such critical moments each person ends up with a uniquely different brain organization.

Violinists who begin their study late in life generally cannot reach virtuoso status because their early brain organization evolves to meet requirements that do not include violin playing. Later learning will still develop special neural pathways but, since they must work around the existing structures, they may be less effective. Learning piano at an early age encourages an organization that allows independent sequencing of the left and right hand. Organ players develop three independent channels for the left hand, the right hand, and the feet (for playing the pedal part). Developing these kinds of abilities late in life can be very difficult.

Figure 10 shows the PET scans[6] from five different individuals all doing the same mental task. The marks, which identify the active parts of the brain, are in different places for each individual. The active areas sometimes even differ in number because each person's brain is spontaneously organized along different paths. With each critical turning point, the brain organization of two people will grow further and further apart so that even identical twins can end up being quite different.

One of the important principles of mathematical chaos theory is "the butterfly effect,"[7] named for a classical example of the major effect of tiny perturbations at the right critical moment: The wind created by the wings of a butterfly in Peking can be the cause of a storm next month in New York. This can happen if the complex chain of events and related global weather systems that ultimately led to the storm in New York was affected by an earlier

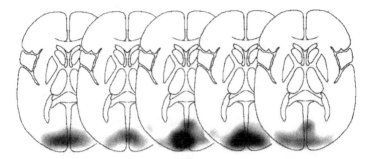

FIGURE 10. PET (positron emission tomography) scans show increases in activity in certain regions of the brain during a specific mental task. Illustration shows that five different subjects doing the same task each have uniquely located active regions. (Thanks to Marcus E. Raichle, Professor of Radiology and Neurology, Department of Neurology and Neurological Surgery, School of Medicine, Washington University, St. Louis, MO.)

storm in Peking that occurred when a tiny breeze from the wing flap of the butterfly at a critical instant began a weather system that turned into a storm.

These critical instants are called bifurcations because one of two paths will be taken. Sometimes these decision points are so delicately balanced that the slightest perturbation will determine the outcome. The final result is like climbing a tree where your decisions at each branching point determine which twig you will finally end up on. When you are partway up the tree you have already eliminated the possibility of reaching some of the twigs.

Major changes in human personality and abilities can likewise be the result of tiny variations in the child's environment at certain critical times. Any new challenge can reinforce and help one of many existing modules evolve, or it can cause a new module to form. Tiny differences in past history or the specific nature of the new challenge can alter the outcome and eventually cause major differences in brain organization.

LANGUAGE DEVELOPMENT

Reading is an important skill that sometimes gets started down the wrong track, causing difficulties later. For example, children who recognize words holistically, as they would recognize other objects, do well reading at a very simple level. As words start getting longer, compound words appear, and spelling becomes a factor, this initially successful strategy becomes a disaster. Reading phonically requires a *new* module, not just adding some words to a module that recognizes things by shape. Dyslexic children have extreme difficulty spelling and often cannot distinguish between the backward spelling of a word and the correct spelling. Whereas in recognizing an object it is important to ignore its orientation (left to right or vice versa), a word written backwards is simply wrong.

Once children start along the wrong path, the longer they continue to use the wrong module, the more firmly ingrained and reinforced it becomes. Remedial exercises that force children to use the correct strategy must start from scratch to train the proper module against strong competition from the module that has the benefit of repeated practice.

Starting down a wrong path in reading has major consequences, so corrective techniques have been developed, but consider all the other areas where a bad pattern can spontaneously organize and cause personality quirks, learning disabilities, and even pathological behavior. At critical moments in a child's development, the spontaneous organization path that prevails can determine brilliance or disability. The highest quality art, literature, and science are usually produced by people who "don't think like the rest of us." The chaotic nature of brain organization thus has both benefits and liabilities.

The critical moments in a child's development are often as difficult to spot as the critical flap of a butterfly's wing. When my father bought me a crystal radio as a gift when he was on a business trip to New York, he didn't know it would so fascinate me that I would develop a technology module that would evolve into an amateur radio module that in turn would evolve into the basis of a career in electronics.

The first time a child tries to steal something is another such critical time. If he succeeds and the behavior is therefore reinforced, it can ultimately develop into a life of crime. Undoing such a development when it is really under way can be extremely difficult, as the crime module can take on a life of its own, quite immune to later stern lectures.

LANGUAGE AND THE LEFT BRAIN

The brain is divided into two mirror-image hemispheres that are virtually identical. In about 95% of the population, speech self-organizes on the left side of the brain. This appears to be a result of a *slight* advantage the left side has for sequenced movements which also predisposes most people to be right-handed (the connections are crossed so the left hemisphere controls the right side of the body and vice versa). Despite this slight advantage, about 5% of the population develops speech on the right side of the brain. Even minor defects in the left side probably tip the balance in favor of the right side in these individuals.

Sometimes an entire defective left hemisphere is surgically removed to prevent it from interfering with the healthy right hemisphere. As long as this surgery is performed before the age of five, normal speech will develop on the right hemisphere. In fact, one case was reported of a college student with a *verbal IQ of 126 who had the left half of his brain removed at the age of five.*[8] This amazing flexibility in the spontaneous organization process allows it simply to work around missing brain tissue.

The basic ability to comprehend sounds of speech begins to organize spontaneously before the child speaks. Recognition of the familiarity of a sound is in itself sufficient for reinforcement learning to occur. A child in China or Japan grows up in a world where the distinction between "L" and "R" sounds is meaningless because their language makes no such distinction. Consequently, the basic phoneme analysis ability that spontaneously organizes does not distinguish between those sounds. When English is learned later, the child is already down an inappropriate path and finds it very difficult to distinguish L from R sounds.[9]

Numerous studies of bilingual children[10] have confirmed that far more than pronunciation is affected if the child initially is exposed to more than one language. The basic organization of the way words are remembered can be affected such that words will be grouped according to meaning, rather than by sound pattern. Though early vocabulary in each language may lag slightly behind single-language children, performance on some nonlinguistic tasks and basic thinking skills has actually been found to improve.

Ideographic languages[11] such as Chinese have no need for an intermediate syllable translation in visually comprehending words so the brain may organize differently for recognizing words. This may make spelling and sounding out words in European languages difficult later. Braille reading must organize with touch rather than vision as the first stage of analysis. Hieroglyphic reading requires yet another organization where meaning varies more with context.

Language is indeed the basis for certain kinds of thought. The vocabulary and organization of our language certainly set the style of our verbal and logical thinking. The sequential nature of Western languages has given the Western nations an advantage in the writing of computer software. The Oriental languages, which use ideograms to represent complete words instead of sequentially building words out of components, may make writing computer programs more difficult because the ability to break down operations into a sequence of tiny steps is less developed. Ideographic languages must certainly change the way the brain spontaneously organizes its vocabulary and may therefore affect the organization of other knowledge.

Once speech is established on the left side of the brain, any module that uses speech or language will tend to spontaneously organize on the left side of the brain because of the more direct connections available to the speech apparatus. Nonverbal modules will then tend to form on the right side of the brain,[12] resulting in a tendency toward left–right specialization of verbal and nonverbal functions.

During early development, speech capability often develops on both sides of the brain. About 10% of all children[13] stutter at some time in their development and then the stuttering clears up in about a year. The problem is worse in boys because they are slower to complete development of the band of nerves linking the left and right halves of the brain. About 15% of normal adults have some speech capability on both sides of their brain.

Stuttering can result when both sides of the brain try to initiate speech at the same time. At the turn of the century stuttering was much more common than it is today. It was finally discovered that about half of the stutterers were people who had been born left-handed but had been forced as children to use their right hand.[14] This unwise practice was confusing the normal development of speech on the same side of the child's brain that controls the dominant hand.

A very clear demonstration that stuttering can result from speech organizing on both sides of the brain is found in a 1966 medical report by Dr. R. K. Jones. He successfully treated four patients[15] who had stuttered since childhood by surgically removing damaged speech areas that had developed on the nondominant side of the brain. Stuttering may well be very similar to what happens when two people both want to speak at the same time: Both may hear the conflict, pause to let the other speak, and then collide again.

DEVELOPMENT OF THE
SELF-CONCEPT

The infant mind begins with no sense of any boundary between its self and the rest of the world. At about the age of 15 months, most babies begin to recognize themselves in a mirror.[16] If a red mark is painted on their nose, they will know enough to wipe it off based on seeing their image in a mirror. They will also react differently to a videotape of themselves than to one showing another baby, indicating a basic understanding of the existence of their self as distinct from others.

At the age of 2, most babies go through a battle with their parents over whether the world will continue to rotate around them. The self boundary, at this age, does not include consideration for other members of the family. By the age of 4, most children have begun to feel at least some merger of their self-interest with that of their mother.

One researcher asked 3- and 4-year-old children, "Where is the part of you that knows your name and thinks about things?" Sixty-four percent of the children localized the thinking part of themselves[17] inside their head (or very close by) and indicated that other people cannot see these activities or the part of the self that performs them. A well-educated Greek in ancient Athens would have pointed to his heart. Clearly this is an example of how quickly our culture loads in the basic software for the self-concept.

Other parts of the self-concept take longer to develop. For example, experiments have shown that most 3-year-olds have not yet developed the belief system that adults use to explain their intentional behavior. They have no concept of beliefs as something separate from their immediate knowledge. In a typical experiment, the child is shown a candy box[18] that actually contains pencils instead of candy. After opening the box, the child is questioned about the belief he had before the box was opened: "When you first saw the box, before we opened it, what did you think was inside it?" One half to two thirds of the 3-year-olds said that they *originally thought there were pencils in the box*. Not having developed a concept of belief as distinct from knowledge, they simply answered with *what they currently knew to be true*. This important part of our self-concept, which adults use so often to explain their actions, seems to be learned by most children at about 4 years of age.

SELF-CONTROL

Self-control requires that the self module be strong enough to prevail over another behavior module. In very small children the self module is not established well enough to achieve control. Before the age of 3 most children cannot successfully stop themselves from doing something by verbal commands. In one experiment children 18 months to 5 years old were given a bulb-squeezing[19] task where they would say "press" and then squeeze a rubber bulb; and then say "don't press" and release it. Children below the age of 3 had no problem with the "press" part of the task, but would actually squeeze the bulb harder on the "don't press" part. Two-year-olds are notoriously difficult to control ("the terrible twos") because they have the physical ability to get into trouble but still lack self-control.

Self-control is learned from parents, friends, and teachers. In a supportive environment, successes are praised and failures are treated as an encouragement to try harder. Some children learn a very negative attitude of helplessness from their parents. This *learned helplessness* can sometimes be undone by utilizing a strong role model to retrain the child to believe in the power of trying harder. It is important, however, for children also to learn to live with their actual limitations, those that no effort can overcome.

The self module undergoes a major upheaval in the teen years as children try to define themselves as separate beings from their parents. Rebellious behavior can often result as a child tries to redefine boundaries and establish an identity separate from the parents. In cultures where the self boundary always includes the extended family the teenage identity crisis, so common in this country, is rare.

The self module continues to evolve throughout life with painful transitions often occurring at points where the self boundary changes. In our society a midlife crisis is often triggered when grown children move away to seek employment, forcing the parents to redefine their self-concept with narrower boundaries.

In cultures where the extended family boundary is a stable lifetime concept these crises are not a problem. Our new concept of the individual self is thus a double-edged sword: It has produced great progress by providing a mobile work force and freeing up individual creativity, but it has also produced some painful side effects by breaking up the unity of the family.

IDENTIFYING YOUR MODULES

The marvel of human uniqueness is that we each end up with a totally distinctive team of specialist modules that ultimately define our personality and abilities. You can learn to recognize your own modules at work through careful observation and some knowledge of evolutionary principles. The cuddling and fighting modules we have already mentioned are fairly universal. We all also have a childish play module that forms in infancy. As we mature and grow old this module usually grows less active; in some people it atrophies completely.

Sometimes you can clearly observe the inconsistency in attitude between the self module, which does advance planning, and this play module: After a fun day of childish play at the beach you would expect enthusiasm two weeks later when making plans to repeat the experience. What you sometimes find is an unfamiliar negative attitude that remembers only that the water was cold and the sand was dirty. Since making future plans is the job of the self module, you are hearing the memory of the day at the beach from the point of view of the self module that is much more concerned with staying warm and clean and therefore may not have had much fun. If you end up back at the beach anyway, again the play module clicks in and you have a wonderful time, ignoring the cold water and messy sand. The same thing can happen when planning a vacation. After almost forcing yourself to go, a moment comes when your self module finally lets go and you begin having a wonderful time in childish play or relaxation.

Another module we all have is a school/work module. This module begins development on the first day of nursery school and gradually evolves as you advance through school. When you finish school and get a job this module continues to evolve to control your working behavior. Graduates of the top universities earn more money not because the specific knowledge they learn but rather because of the behavior and work habits they have developed give them an advantage on the job. They have developed both their self module and a school/work module that knows how to work hard and succeed.

Sibling relationships also tend to develop independent patterns: The arrival of a new little brother or sister is one of those crucial moments in a child's life when a new module may or may not form. The attitude of that module can be positive or negative, depending on very subtle factors. In adulthood, if the sibling is no longer present the module may resurface in some other relationship at work or in a marriage where the context is similar enough to make that module prevail.

Favorite childhood games and pastimes can sometimes develop into a unique module that evolves into related adult behavior patterns. Dangerous childhood games, for example, can later evolve into pleasurable hobbies such as skiing or rock climbing or into pathological patterns such as serial murder, gambling, or burglary. A generous caregiver module or a mommy module may evolve from playing with dolls. Relaxed behavior on camping trips or when fishing may evolve from similar times in childhood and may be totally different from frantically driven business behavior that has its genesis at exam times in high school or college.

Binge behavior may also have its origins early in childhood. Some overweight people seem to have a binge module that takes control during the first piece of pie and effectively changes their personality. The cautious dieting of their normal self-controlled behavior gives way to out of control eating, which ends only when they are sick or out of pie. Bulimics end this pattern by vomiting up what they have eaten. The binge module has a life of its own and can develop quite a different personality. Drunks, for example, often have a mean brutal personality that is clearly recognizable when they have lost control.

Work skills and hobbies also usually develop into unique modules. A piano player can continue playing a song while another module simultaneously holds a conversation about a request for another song. During many skilled jobs other modules are free to have conversations, thoughts, and daydreams while the work is in progress.

Almost all of us have a module for driving a car that makes it possible to independently hold a conversation or do intensive thinking while driving. Some people have a driving personality that is obviously distinct from their normal personality. Gentle people sometimes have an aggressive personality that gets engaged during driving. That personality may show anger by tailgating and cutting off other cars, giving the finger, and even cursing. If someone cuts them off, a pleasant conversation may be interrupted by a string of obscenities from the driving module, which has a distinctly different sound and attitude.

Not all modules have the ability to control speech. Some are able to work on a problem and pass the results to other modules through intermodule connections. When you suddenly realize the solution to a problem or remember a name without having been aware of thinking about it, the work is clearly done by a nonverbal module working in parallel. Any kind of interconnection structure that works is possible in a spontaneously organized system, so modules can overlap, communicate, and cooperate in many ways.

Though it may be difficult to identify your specific nonverbal modules, you can certainly learn to make better use of them. All creative people learn to respect and work with these powerful modules even though they are invisible to consciousness.

One such technique is called "incubation": Once you have reached an impasse in solving a difficult problem, you simply put it aside and work on something else while your unconscious modules continue working on the problem. Often the key to the problem will be revealed to you in a flash later as some unknown module passes its answer through intermodule communications channels. The more this kind of thinking is practiced, the more reinforced and developed it becomes.

CHAPTER TEN

Nonverbal Thinking

All credibility, all good conscience, all evidence of truth come only from the senses.
—— *Nietzsche, 1886*

A poem...begins as a lump in the throat, a sense of wrong, a homesickness, a lovesickness. . . . It finds the thought and the thought finds the words.
—— *Robert Frost, 1916*

Most Experiences are unsayable, they happen in a space that no word has ever entered.
—— *Rilke, 1903*

Since the brain is insensitive to pain, brain surgery is often done with the patient fully conscious. A local anesthetic is used only on the flesh of the scalp around a circular "trap door" that is cut in the skull for access. This makes it possible for the surgeon to converse with the patient throughout the operation and monitor the effects of the surgery. Sometimes tumors or severe epilepsy make it necessary to remove surgically an entire half of the brain in an operation called a hemispherectomy. One surgeon's report on the removal of the entire right half of the brain on four patients stated that, "Conversation with the patients was carried on throughout the surgery *without any significant change in conscious state.*"[1] Clearly the patient's self module failed to notice the removal of all of the modules in the other half of the brain! Since we have already shown that the self handles discussion of consciousness even though it has no direct awareness of the other modules, this is not surprising. In fact, the surgeon could probably continue cutting and remove everything, down to the self module and its supporting speech apparatus, and the patient would continue the conversation as though nothing was happening.

The self module's awareness of other modules comes, not from direct access, but from observation. After the operation, the patient may find that half of his body is paralyzed and that he cannot put his clothes on rightside-up or find his way back to his bed. The self will typically continue to try to rationalize these obvious deficits with confabulations, like the press secretary trying to keep things together. The emotional aspects of the patient's personality may also disappear, but the self module will often continue, cheerfully, making light of the situation.

WORDS: USEFUL BUT DANGEROUS

Words are both powerful and dangerous. They are the language of certain kinds of logical thought and knowledge. Even more important, words are the medium with which we communicate the concepts of self and our experience of consciousness. Because of this, it is easy to fool yourself into thinking that all thought is expressed in words. The truth is, *most of your thoughts and most of your knowledge are in nonverbal form* and, therefore, are unconscious and invisible.

We have defined the self module as the one that uses introspection to describe verbally our thoughts, consciousness, and feelings. If your self-concept includes the belief that all thoughts are in words, then consciousness will convincingly confirm that belief. Here we will try to alter that belief to one that better correlates with the reality of how the mind actually functions. With practice, you can learn to modify your conscious experience so that it also includes the richness of nonverbal thinking. This can significantly increase your pleasure in life and allow you to develop abilities you never thought possible.

Your brain's only job is to process sensory inputs and respond by producing movement. Movement is, in fact, the *only* useful result of the brain's activity: Thought by itself is useless until it is expressed by some kind of movement such as physical action, speech, writing, or keyboard entry. In our evolution from lower animals, refinements, such as language and verbal thought, were simply added on top of the existing structures that generate movement. Internal, verbal thought that evolved from speech was a separate, late addition, not a replacement for sensory thinking. Nonverbal thinking has continued to evolve and still does the majority of the mind's work, using nonverbal knowledge directly to solve problems and generate movement. When you are proficient in sports or dance, your thoughts are not in words but rather in the form of kinesthetic images.

When we try to analyze and understand our thoughts, the result is *always* in words. This one-sided view, which ignores all of the nonverbal aspects, gives us a distorted view of our thinking and knowledge. For example, if we recall a conversation, we will probably retell only the words even though a major part of human communications is nonverbal. It has been estimated that words carry only 7%[2] of the total feeling communicated, while 38% is inflection and the remaining 55% is communicated in the form of facial and body expression. Silent movies and mimes demonstrate just how much can be communicated without words.

While listening to a tragic aria from an Italian opera, you may cry—even though you have no idea what the words mean. Deprived of words, you will have difficulty describing why you are crying. If the aria was in English, you would easily explain your tears by repeating some of the sad lyrics. Words, so much easier to verbalize than the nonverbal communications, tend to hog the spotlight when we try to explain our feelings and behavior. When we listen to vocal music in a foreign language, we are forced to pay more attention to the other powerful communications we are experiencing in the gesture and tone of the voice. When we listen to a recording, we are also deprived of the visual communications of facial expression and body language—and yet again, a sad aria in Italian can make us cry. In the old days, people were certainly moved to tears by the silent movies. Without words grabbing the spotlight, people became more sensitive to facial expressions and body language.

Verbal comprehension is performed by a different module than the one that judges emotional expression from tone of voice. This is confirmed by studying patients after a stroke or brain injury: Many people retain their ability to comprehend the cold, logical meaning of language yet lose their ability to respond to the emotional expression. In normal people there is competition between these two modes: When we can't understand the lyrics, the emotional side wins control. When we do understand the lyrics, we tend to explain our feelings by interpreting the verbal meaning even when our reaction is primarily from the nonverbal inputs.

Our interactions with other people all seem to be unified because language hogs the spotlight. However, all conversations are, in reality, interactions between many different modules working in parallel. Body language, facial expressions, and tone of voice are extremely important parts of any conversations that may be controlled by a module other than the one controlling speech. They are often ignored during verbal recall. Television reproduces all of these modes of communications, making it much more powerful than print media, which is limited to words only.

With practice you can increase your self module's awareness of nonverbal communications. A good way to practice without driving your friends crazy is to watch dramatic shows on television with the sound turned off. Watch the facial gestures without the distraction of words and try to notice the subtle movements of eyes, eyebrows, mouth, hands, and the body gestures that any good actor uses. Notice that the two sides of people's mouths are often out of sync because each is controlled by a different side of the brain. Often involuntary emotional expressions are more obvious on the left side of the mouth while intentional ones are stronger on the right.

Good businessmen know that written communications and even E-mail can easily get a negotiation off track and even produce anger because it is easy for the reader to get a wrong meaning from the words alone. Talking on the telephone or voice mail at least adds the subtle messages of tone of voice and inflection. It is often worth an expensive airline ticket just to talk to a person face to face so that meaning can be reinforced by interactions of body language and facial expression.

NONVERBAL CONSCIOUSNESS

The convenience of words can obscure an important component of our own experience of consciousness. Words are used to define the very meaning of consciousness: in the dictionary, in philosophical and psychological discussions, and even in this book. Our false belief in the power of verbal introspection causes us to imagine a complete mental world built on words.

H. D. Barlow[3] of Cambridge University wrote:

> It is argued that consciousness primarily arises in the relation between one individual and another, and is not a property of a brain in isolation. One can, of course, be conscious when one is alone, but it is suggested that on these occasions one is rehearsing future discourse with an imagined individual. ... Thus the survival value of consciousness consists of a peculiar form of gregarious behavior it generates in man; it is nature's trick to chain him to the herd.

There is, however, another kind of consciousness that uses no words. Stroke patients can have large parts of their brain damaged by loss of blood circulation. Those who completely lose their powers of logical speech provide a clear demonstration of consciousness without words. Though unable to speak about it, they are clearly still conscious, with their nonverbal personality and knowledge intact. Though their self module is essentially dead, they defiantly remain conscious. The kind of consciousness they feel is present in all of us, but it tends to get upstaged by the easy verbalization of the self module.

Some brain tumor patients have even had the entire left hemisphere surgically removed. Though they lost all logical speech ability, they remained conscious and retained their personality characteristics such as humor, boredom, love, and frustration.[4] With the self module removed and speech destroyed much of what we call a "person" still remains. We can all benefit if we can learn to see beyond the smoke screen of verbal introspection and experience our nonverbal consciousness directly.

One of the reasons we are so easily confused about consciousness is that our language tries to use that single word for a wide range of meanings. In Sanskrit, the ancient Indian language, there are some 20 different words[5] for various forms of consciousness. Clearly the self module has a specific kind of consciousness that is verbal and self-reflective. It is aware of and can reflect on its own existence. When the self module is in control we are self-conscious because that is the specialty of the self. Other modules have their own kind of consciousness. We all have a childish play module that is not self-conscious and can consciously experience the simple joy of playing like a small child. Another kind of consciousness is the quiet intensity you feel when you are deeply absorbed in a nonverbal task. Yet another is the pleasant glow you feel when cuddling with the one you love. A balanced personality retains the ability to enjoy all of these forms of consciousness. Many people have lost touch with them by allowing a takeover by their misunderstanding self module to invalidate them.

CREATIVE THINKING

All creative thinking makes extensive use of non-verbal modes of thought. We can all improve our creativity by learning how to use these nonverbal modules effectively. In 1945 Jacques Hadamard[6] sent questionnaires to prominent mathematicians all over America to learn the secrets of their creative success. He summarized the results:

> Practically all of them . . . avoid not only the use of mental words but also the mental use of algebraic or other precise signs . . . The mental pictures of the mathematicians whose answers I have received are most frequently visual, but they may be of another kind—for instance, kinetic.

It is interesting that even though our schools teach very little that is not verbal, the most successful people in the very logical field of mathematics don't think in words. They have developed these nonverbal modules to such a degree that they depend on them.

Albert Einstein was one of the most creative geniuses of all time. His answer to Hadamard's survey shows that he not only used nonverbal thinking but also had a conscious awareness of these kinds of thoughts. He wrote:

> (A) The words of language, as they are written or spoken, do not seem to play any role in my mechanism of thought. The physical entities which seem to serve as elements in thought are certain signs and more or less clear images which can be "voluntarily" reproduced and combined.
>
> There is, of course, a certain connection between those elements and the relevant logical concepts. It is also clear that the desire to arrive finally at logically connected concepts is the emotional basis of this rather vague play with the above mentioned ele-

ments. But taken from a psychological viewpoint, this comminatory play seems to be the essential feature in productive thought—before there is any connection with logical construction in words or other kinds of signs which can be communicated to others.

(B) The above mentioned elements are, in my case, of visual and some of muscular type. Conventional words or other signs have to be sought for laboriously only in a secondary stage, when the mentioned associative play is sufficiently established and can be reproduced at will.

Words are too restrictive to be the basis for creative thought but are used only *after* the creative breakthrough. Since classes in school are taught in words, this ability to think in nonverbal images was apparently learned outside of school by these great thinkers. Even Aristotle, the genius who first formalized the rules of logic, thought in nonverbal images. In *De Anima* he wrote: "It is impossible even to think without a mental picture. The same affection is involved in thinking as in drawing a diagram."

Though many of our modules with powers of speech can be deduced by watching our behavior, nonverbal modules are much harder to identify. We can see from the results that some modules can be working on a problem while we are consciously doing something else. If we get stuck on a problem like remembering a name, the module that remembers names clearly continues wrestling with the problem because, even though we are busy with something else, we suddenly get a strange feeling and bingo! We have the name. Clearly there are links between some modules that allow this kind of information to be passed.

IMPROVING YOUR CREATIVITY

Creative people learn to put this parallel processing to work in an organized way. In a 1945 book titled *The Art of Thought*, G. Wallas broke the creative process into four stages: preparation, incubation, illumination, and verification. In the *preparation* stage relevant information is gathered and the problem is narrowed down until the obstacles are visible. Once this is done you can work on something else while the *incubation* step is performed outside of your awareness. It is permissible to occasionally think about the problem during this stage but there should be no pressure for a solution. With some luck the *illumination* stage will come when the results of subconscious thinking present themselves as an insight or intuition. Finally, in the *verification* stage you logically test the intuition for validity and express the final solution in verbal form.

This kind of creative thinking process improves with practice because your confidence in the unconscious thinking of the incubation stage gives those modules a chance to develop. Once you develop that confidence you can learn to relax and remove the pressure for a solution that can block creativity. Many complex problems are not solved by a single intuition but require you to identify the next level of difficulties and start the incubation step again. Really productive thinkers often overlap their projects like a juggler: They work on the definition or verification stage of one problem while another problem is in the incubation stage.

The important principle here is to let the specialist modules do what they do best. Logical thinking is good for identifying problems and for testing the validity of intuitive insights, but it is not good for making creative breakthroughs. The reason the modules that are good at these creative leaps are nonverbal is that language is too tightly structured to be good for creative thought. Nonverbal images have a vagueness that lends itself to the flexibility required for making the distant connections between unrelated things that are the basis of most creative breakthroughs. Computers are not creative because they are too literal.

One of the most famous intuitive leaps in history was when Archimedes discovered the principle that now bears his name. His protector had given him a gold crown that he was suspected to be adulterated with silver, and Archimedes was asked to tell him if it was real. Archimedes knew that, since gold is heavier than silver, he could solve the problem if he could just find a way to measure the volume of the crown. As he sat in his bathtub, the water level rose as he had seen it do hundreds of times. This time Archimedes recognized the rising water as the solution to his problem: The volume of the water that was displaced was equal to the volume of his immersed body. "Eureka!" he cried as he jumped out of the tub and ran through the streets naked.

Talented people develop specialized modules that are the key to their success yet are not directly accessible to the introspection of their self module. These modules produce miraculous works of art that the artist can only attempt to describe verbally. Artists' verbal descriptions of their paintings are probably no more accurate than the descriptions of any art critic because both the artist's self module and the critic are looking at the painting as an outsider.

Mozart described the apparently subconscious process of his musical compositions in a famous letter[7]:

> When I feel well and in a good humor, or when I am taking a drive or walking after a good meal, or in the night when I cannot sleep, thoughts crowd into my mind as easily as you could wish. Whence and how do they come? I do not know and I have nothing to do with it. Those which please me I keep in my head and hum them: at least others have told me that I do so. Once I have my theme another melody comes, linking itself to the first one, in accordance with the needs of the composition as a whole: the counterpoint, the part of each instrument, and all those melodic fragments at last produce the entire work.

When the composition was complete in his head, Mozart often wrote down the notes directly from the musical image in his head. Sometimes he would have his wife read a book to him to occupy his mind while he wrote out the notes in his head.

THE REPTILIAN BRAIN

Language ability is a recent addition to our brain in evolutionary terms. Since evolution never has the luxury of redesign, old structures must always remain intact and functional while new ones, like language, evolve to add refinement. As evolution added these new structures to the reptilian brain the result was modification and elaboration rather than a replacement of the primitive reptilian behavior patterns. As evolution continues the new structures can gradually take over and replace the old, but they must compete to do so. We are all born with a repertoire of instinctive behavior patterns that still affect our behavior. The spontaneously organized modules of the more recently evolved parts of our brain can only inhibit, refine, or elaborate on these patterns.

The fixed behavior patterns of reptiles are often visible through the thin veneer of human behavior. American neurophysiologist Paul MacLean enumerated 24 different instinctive reptilian behavior[8] patterns, including: (1) *selection and preparation of homesite;* (2) *establishment of domain or territory;* (5) *showing place-preferences;* (6) *ritualistic display in defense of territory, commonly involving the use of coloration and adornments;* (7) *formalized intraspecific fighting in defense of territory;* (8) *triumphal display in successful defense;* (9) *assumption of distinctive postures and coloration in signaling surrender;* (10) *routinization of daily activities;* (11) *foraging;* (12) *hunting;* (13) *homing;* (14) *hoarding;* (15) *use of defecation posts;* (16)*formation of social groups;* (17) *establishment of social hierarchy by ritualistic display and other means;* (18) *greeting;* (19) *"grooming";* (20) *courtship with displays using coloration and adornments;* (21) *breeding and, in isolated instances, attending offspring;* (23) *flocking;* and (24) m*igration.*

Experiments with monkeys have confirmed that their sexual display behavior can be eliminated only by removing parts of the lower reptilian portion of their brain. Destruction of more recently evolved parts of their brain leaves sexual display behavior intact. In fact, a human male paraplegic, paralyzed by a severed spinal cord, can still have an erection if his penis is stroked.[9] The spinal cord, though completely disconnected from the brain, has its own primitive behavior program. Though the self module does an amazingly good job of fulfilling our false belief that it controls everything, penile erection is one area where this fiction sometimes becomes painfully obvious: A penis sometimes seems to have a mind of its own for a good reason—it does. The other reptilian behavior patterns on the list above also probably live on as the driving forces in human behavior to which verbal introspection has no access.

If you watch carefully, you can see primitive behavior patterns showing through our civilized veneer at business meetings, cocktail parties, sporting events, on battlefields, and in many other common settings. Self-control often really means that the logical self module has seized control and substituted rational, verbally directed behavior for more primitive responses. Only when this occurs does introspection really give us access to the thoughts that cause our actions.

Though self-control can often prevent fights and other destructive behavior, too much control is not the way to lead a happy and meaningful life. *The basic drives that we have inherited from lower animals help give meaning and feeling to life*. To prove this to yourself make a list of the things that give you the most pleasure in life and then analyze each item to find the basic drive it satisfies. Total self-control means existing like a human computer with nothing but logic controlling your behavior. The real goal should be to evolve and refine your basic drives so that they may safely be allowed to rule more rather than less. By bringing your self module into harmony with these basic drives you can reduce internal conflict and bring more meaning to life. Your self module can guide and support these basic behaviors, as a wise CEO would guide and support the specialists within a corporation. Pushing them aside and overriding them only stifles their development and makes them frustrated and unruly. Successful corporate presidents often "go with their gut" when making decisions.

NONVERBAL LOGIC

What the philosophers and mathematicians call logic is a completely verbal game with verbal rules. Nonverbal thinking has its own kind of logic, which can often be more effective than verbal logic. Kinesthetic logic, for example, is the only effective way to perform sports and dance movements. Nonverbal kinesthetic knowledge of body and ball dynamics is used directly to solve problems instantly. Catching a ball in a crosswind requires complex solving of trajectory problems with wind correction, which would be impossible if we used equations and verbal logic. Amateurs often try to override this highly effective kinesthetic logic with verbal logic, producing disastrous results. Lawyers and engineers are notoriously bad dancers because their highly developed and overconfident logical self module tends to win the competition for control.

People with highly developed logical thinking are also often handicapped in art, sports, and music. A good artist utilizes visual thinking to think directly in images, using nonverbal knowledge. Art education often misses this point by trying to teach verbal concepts, making matters worse. Formulas for body proportions are a perfect example: Though counting the number of head lengths between the knee and the ground may be a good way to *check* proportions, thinking in terms of verbal rules while drawing or sculpting can often engage the wrong module, ruining the result.

One excellent art teaching program based on Betty Edwards' excellent book *Drawing on the Right Side of the Brain* forces people to copy drawings *upside down*: This puts logical control at a disadvantage, forcing it to release its grip. Many people on this program have had amazing breakthroughs—allowing the artist inside them finally to emerge. Music is another area wherein verbal logic can stifle the artist inside, producing a mechanical, player piano pianist who has no ability but to read notes on paper. Good musicians think directly in musical sound images, to compose and play by ear. Musical logic makes it possible for many people to compose with no knowledge of the verbal rules of harmony and composition.

THE LOGIC OF EMOTIONS

Our emotions and feelings also have their own kind of logic, which is not easily verbalized because it operates without words. When we criticize a movie, book, or play because the characters don't seem real, we mean that their emotions aren't logical. We can often agree on such criticisms, thus proving that there is a generally agreed logic to emotions.[10] When we say, "She wouldn't have reacted that way," we mean that the character violated the rules of emotional logic.

Our own emotional logic sometimes makes us do things that seem strange and illogical. Further analysis can usually uncover an underlying cause, such as a previous painful experience, which makes the behavior quite logical from an emotional standpoint. Emotional logic is driven by our need to *maximize self-esteem and personal dignity*. This can sometimes conflict with long-term goals set by the self module and make emotion-driven actions seem illogical. For example: You are trapped in a job you hate, you allow yourself the luxury of revealing this to your boss, and it results in your getting fired. This certainly interferes with your logical long-term plan for success, but it is a perfectly logical action for preserving your self-esteem.

Emotions come from the older structures of the brain. *Long-term planning is a uniquely human capability that is based on the newer, language-based parts of the brain.* Chimpanzees and other nonhumans live a completely reactive life without any long-term planning. Though they can throw things, they never systematically *practice* throwing, as even a child[11] can do. It is not surprising then that our emotional logic is sometimes at odds with the long-term plans of the self module. Many emotional and physical illnesses are the result of stress caused by our logical self module overriding our natural emotional logic. Destructive emotional outbursts occur when the pressure, resulting from this override, builds to an intolerable level.

Emotional reactions often seem illogical because we try to explain them by using verbal introspection. Though we think we are speaking with authority, our explanations are really nothing more than creative theorizing, which is often totally incorrect. The self module has no direct access to our emotional logic, which is based on feelings, not words. Our own theories about the reasons for our emotional responses are often less reliable than those of an outside observer. Whatever we decide about the reasons for our actions is sure to be convincingly confirmed by our creative perception.

The popular notion that we cannot be mistaken about our own feelings is based on the false assumption that "we" is a single entity. The truth is that *the self module is often dead wrong about the cause of our feelings and often even misidentifies them.* For example, it is quite common to say that we hate someone when, in reality, we love them. Friends can see it and, after time has passed, we will often admit it, but at the time we insist on misidentifying the feeling.[12] We may feel anger toward the cat when we are really angry with our boss. Or, we may deny that we are angry when our anger is obvious to any impartial observer. We may think that we are depressed when, in reality, we are angry. It is rare for anybody to admit to jealousy or envy, though they are common emotions. Even basic feelings like heat and cold can be confused under certain conditions: If you show someone a blowtorch, then secretly put ice on their hand, they will think that you have burned them. The problem with understanding emotions is that they originate outside the self module. The self, a logical, language-oriented module, does its best to contrive a story that rationalizes all behavior.

How can we get more "in touch" with our emotions? Unfortunately, there is no easy answer, but a good start is to realize that the self module is an outside observer of emotions. Open your mind to the possibility that false beliefs can cause a convincing illusion of direct understanding of the reasons for your emotional behavior. Having faced these facts, you are then ready to *feel* your emotions with the nonverbal part of your consciousness. Don't expect them to be articulate. Joy is simply joy and pain is simply pain. The fine distinctions are all things you will have to fabricate with words and the feelings surely will suffer in the translation. If you want to theorize about the reasons, do it as you would for a friend—with the full realization that the words are coming from an observer.

FLOW: SILENCING THE SELF MODULE

The self module, like a loudmouth who monopolizes the conversation, drowns out important parts of our consciousness that feel things but cannot talk about them. With effort, we can develop our awareness of this important, but silent, part of our being. Long before the modular concept of brain organization was proposed, people with an intuitive understanding developed techniques for silencing the self.

For centuries, Eastern religions have taught that belief in individual selfhood is an illusion. The goal of Sufi practice is to reach the ecstatic state of *fana*, or freedom from the self.[13] Zen Buddhism is based on denial of the relevance of self. Yoga, Taoism, and the Oriental martial arts are all, in their authentic form, focused on silencing the self.

All of the exercises that have been developed for silencing the self module involve focusing the mind on something in the present. Future planning is a verbal, step-by-step process, so future planning and goals must be avoided. To really *feel* life, we must live in the present. In meditation, the focus is sometimes on a single word (mantra) and sometimes on basic functions such as breathing. Sometimes the focus is on some activity such as T'ai Chi, karate movements, or yoga body postures. A common practice with all techniques is to become totally absorbed in nonverbal activity, thus preventing the self module from gaining control. When this *flow state* is achieved, time flies and worries disappear. The nagging by the self module about things you "should do" ceases and is replaced by a feeling of bliss.

Instead of concentrating on rationalistic planning and working toward goals, which are the job of the self, Yoga teaches one to focus on physical activities that would normally be automatic. Activities such as movement, eating, breathing, or digesting are done consciously and deliberately. Monks in Zen monasteries are encouraged to focus solely on their required chores. When washing the floor, the mind should be focused on the washing movements themselves, not on how nice the floor will look when it is done or on how much is left to do. Nor are you supposed to daydream or think about what you will do later on. When the allotted time for a chore is up, the monk simply moves onto the next task, whether or not the job is completed. This rule helps prevent goal-oriented thinking, which would engage the self. Zen spiritual exercises punish rational thinking for the same reason: It encourages the self module to take control.

USING SPORTS AND CRAFTS

Mental discipline is difficult for some people, but there are other ways to achieve a flow state.[14] Danger, or the appearance of danger, focuses the mind without need for discipline. Sports such as skiing, mountain climbing, hang gliding, and car racing silence the self module nicely. Even if the fear is of nothing more than pleasantly falling into the water, sports such as windsurfing and waterskiing require careful attention and are therefore good for silencing the self. Games such as tennis, handball, or volleyball requiring fast reflexes for effective play can also be good, if played with kinesthetic thinking. Running can silence the self module by pushing the body's endurance to a point where all attention is focused on the act of running.

Arts and crafts, when done correctly, use intense nonverbal thinking. Sculpture, for example, requires thinking directly in tactile and visual images. While sculpting, one goes into a wonderful flow state where time seems to fly by, like being unconscious. Of course, the self module later reports unconsciousness because it has not been in control. The consciousness we feel when absorbed in a nonverbal task is the primitive kind that other animals probably feel. Some art students never experience this quieting of the mind because their logical self module never lets go. The work they produce is usually poor. Breaking the hold of the self module during activities that should be nonverbal is a real problem for some people. However, once they have a breakthrough in one area, allowing the self module to let go in other areas becomes easier. Each person has an area where breakthrough will be easiest.

Schools should make it a goal to ensure that every child learns how to do something in a nonverbal state. Unfortunately, music, art, and sports are always the first things cut back to balance school budgets. They don't directly affect academic achievement tests, but they do develop important nonverbal thinking skills and also teach the child how to experience the joy of nonverbal consciousness. This is an important example of how human potential can be wasted when we misunderstand how the mind really works.

People who don't know how to silence their self module with flow activities generally do it with television: Staring at a television set is an easy way to engage your attention and therefore silence the self. Violent action shows with dangerous car chases engage the attention of our nonverbal side just as participating in dangerous sports does. Though certainly effective at silencing the self, watching passively does little to develop our ability to *use* nonverbal thinking. Some people become addicted to spending entire weekends watching sports on television. It may be the only way they know to silence their self module.

Workaholics, having given up even trying to silence their self, remain engaged in self-directed behavior all of their waking hours. Society benefits from these people because, although they may get ulcers or heart attacks from overwork, they are the driving force in our tremendous technical progress. Unfortunately for them, the evolutionary forces that drive the development of our culture's self-concept tend to select for progress, not personal happiness. Some lucky people in low-stress, absorbing jobs can work, like the Zen monks, in a flow state for their allotted working hours.

DEVELOPING SENSUOUS THINKING

A well-balanced person has a strong self module *and* strong nonverbal modules. The education we have received has damaged the nonverbal side in most of us. With sustained effort we can undo much of this damage. However, it takes years to change mental habits that have been reinforced for decades. In order to develop your nonverbal side, your self module must exercise control and learn to intentionally stand back to nurture this development. Whenever we try to verbalize things, we take away from our direct sensuous experience. Many academic classes in art and music use too many words. The words stand in the way of direct nonverbal appreciation or performance. We can use our senses to put us into a flow state if we can just quiet the self module and allow our sensuous feelings to take control. We usually associate the word *sensuous* with sex. Indeed, making love is one way that most people can experience the senses. However, sensuous thinking doesn't require the privacy of your bedroom. It can be a major part of your life, bringing meaning and pleasure often throughout the day.

If you have difficulty letting go and allowing your feelings to emerge, you are not alone. Our culture buries sensuous thinking in an avalanche of words. A good way to start relearning these habits is to practice paying attention to your senses. Remember, there is a competition between modules, so if you can focus your attention on *one sense at* a time, you will maximize your chances of success. Vision is such an important sense that it tends to overwhelm the other senses. Blind people, as is commonly known, develop their senses of hearing, touch, and smell to incredible levels because they lack this competition. You can do the same by simply closing your eyes or using a blindfold.

One good method is to focus on *really feeling* just one sense at a time, directly, and, without analysis, to allow a simple, nonverbal consciousness of feeling to take over. For example, focus on your sense of touch by feeling like a mute, blind sculptor. With closed eyes, caress sensuously shaped objects like rocks, sculptures, and even people as a sculptor would, forming a tactile image in your mind. Learn to *know* a shape with just your hands—as a sightless person would. Take your time and really become acquainted with every detail of surface texture, shape, and even temperature. Remember, no visual images or words are allowed. If you want to pursue this further, take a sculpture class: Learning to sculpt in clay can really help you develop this ability. You will soon learn to think directly in tactile images and your perception of shapes will be changed forever.

When you were an infant, your whole world was experienced through your mouth. A baby tastes and feels everything to become acquainted with the world, and you still have that behavior buried beneath the layers of "civilized" thought. A real gourmet experiences food in that way. Each grain of rice has a wonderful shape that can be felt with the tongue as you eat. The aroma of the food under your nose and inside your mouth is something you can appreciate if you just focus your attention. Wine experts swirl the wine in the glass, inhale the bouquet, and then taste. They allow the wine to curl around their tongue to feel its texture and bring out the bouquet inside their mouth. Sensitivity to the senses is a matter of paying attention. It can be developed with a little effort, or it can be lost in the chaotic buzz of words.

Sound can be another source of sensuous pleasure. When you are standing in the woods, close your eyes and listen to the wind in the trees, to the birds, and even to the buzzing of insects. Feel the wind caress your skin. Canned music is often too available, assaulting us everywhere from elevators to supermarkets. We soon become desensitized and stop paying attention. Try to deprive yourself of sound for as long as possible, until the numbness dissipates. Then get comfortable, close your eyes, and *really listen* to music, like a cave man who has never heard music before—using just your feelings.

In these days of television and magazines our sense of vision also becomes saturated. It is easy to forget how to *really look* at things. Here again, a blindfold can be helpful. After depriving yourself of vision, try to really look at things as if your vision was just restored by a miraculous operation. Learn to observe things like an artist and appreciate every nuance of color, light, and texture. Before you eat a dinner, enjoy the visual treat of the food's colors and textures. Do like the wine experts and spend some time really paying attention to the visual beauty of the wine before you drink it.

Please remember that exercises like these cannot permanently change the way you perceive things. Your habits of perception, etched in by a lifetime, will not change in an hour. What practice can do is open your mind to the joy of sensuous thinking so that you can spend the rest of your life working toward changing those habits. Your self module can learn to stand back and let the other parts of you develop and gain strength. Instead of being a tyrant that tries to take over everything, your self module can become the supportive spokesperson for a happy family of confident specialists.

A fundamental change in a basic belief is called a paradigm shift. One of the most famous paradigm shifts was the Copernican revolution, in which the Earth-centered concept of the universe gave way to the realization that the Earth was simply one of many planets revolving around the sun. We must now undergo a similar change in belief and realize that the self module is just one of many powerful and useful modules in our mind.

CHAPTER ELEVEN

Love
Merging the Self

Love is a gift of oneself.
—— Jean Anouilh, 1948

The heart has its reasons which reason knows nothing of.
—— Blaise Pascal, 1656

Nothing demonstrates the practical application of the ideas we have been discussing more clearly than the love relationship. It is one area of our lives where primitive emotions can collide most dramatically with the logic of our beliefs. Love involves a redefinition of the boundaries of our self module to include another person. This can be a frightening or even impossible task if your self module is insecure or accustomed to fighting for survival. Differences in the self-concept between lovers can cause them to interpret the world in totally different and conflicting ways.

The very idea of love is a concept learned from our culture along with the other concepts that constitute the self. In other cultures and other times, the concept of love, and therefore the experience of love, is and was completely different. Yet love has a biological basis, honed by evolution, with survival forces acting differently on men than on women. I am devoting an entire chapter to love because it is a specific example of the complex interaction between the mind's evolutionary history and the learned concepts of our self. The mental illusions of our belief system are nowhere more clearly demonstrated than in love relationships. In love, as in all of our mental software, if we can harmonize our concepts with the underlying primitive drives we can maximize happiness and minimize frustration.

During the first few months in the womb male and female babies are virtually identical. In the third month of development the genital area of both sexes consists of an open groove like a female. After the fourth month, if masculine hormones are present, this groove grows closed[1] and the testicles descend. The fine line (raphé) down the center of the scrotum and penis is the result of this last-minute joining. The sex hormones also cause important changes in the brain that give men and women somewhat different instinctive behavior.

THE BIOLOGICAL BASIS OF LOVE

Since the human infant is so helpless during the first years of its life, a bonding system has evolved to provide for the child's survival. The awkwardness of pregnancy and the demands of nursing made it important for sexual bonds to evolve that would keep human couples together in a kind of symbiotic relationship that improved the infant's chance of survival. As with any such relationship, the two symbionts coevolve so that they complement each other.

Most of our evolution occurred in a wild hunter-gathering existence. A man who impregnated as many women as possible could maximize the survival of his genes, while a woman had to be more stable and take care of the infant for her genes to survive. After millions of years of evolution, we can see the results in the differing attitudes of men and women.[2] Surveys in the United States and anthropological studies[3] of other cultures have shown that men tend to rate *good looks* first in their priorities for choosing a mate. While this sounds shallow, in evolutionary terms good looks means a healthy look, which favors a healthy mother and child. The same studies find that women rate *being a good provider* as the number one trait they seek in a man. Sounding equally shallow, this also makes sense, in evolutionary terms, because it ensures that the man will be able to provide the support needed so that the woman's child can survive.

Though only 3% of mammals bond for life, humans have special needs, which are related to the long period of complete helplessness of infants. Women are the only mammals receptive to intercourse all of the time rather than just during estrus.[4] This helps make monogamy work by making it unnecessary for the man to go elsewhere for sex. Several studies indicate that *over 90% of all people in all societies marry at some point in their lives*.[5] Though the majority of the world's cultures allow men to take more than one wife,[6] only about 5–10% of the men in those cultures actually take multiple wives. Thus, the vast majority of men worldwide marry only one female at a time.

Though culture has a strong effect on the nature of male–female bonding, strong support is also provided by biology. Our basic emotional makeup produces a strong bonding force during and after sexual intercourse. Sexual penetration is indeed a merging of *physical* self-boundaries. The intensity of such closeness can have a transforming effect on emotional self-boundaries. In species where male–female bonding does not exist, the sexual act is never prolonged or ritualistic. After being serviced by the rooster, a hen simply shakes her feathers and resumes pecking her feed as he moves on.

The euphoric feeling during human lovemaking is caused by a release of endorphins and supported by increases in the euphoria-producing chemical phenylethylamine (PEA) in the bloodstream. One researcher, studying depression, found high levels of this chemical in the urine of 33 people who were happily attached to a significant other and said they were feeling great. The two subjects going through a divorce had very low PEA levels.[7] When we crave a love relationship we may really just be looking for a PEA fix.

SMELL AND SEXUAL CHEMISTRY

Our senses of smell and touch have the longest evolutionary history and therefore the most direct effect on our feelings. That unconscious sexual chemistry, which seems so mysterious to our logical mind, is probably based on primitive reactions to smell that aren't even acknowledged by our consciousness. Any dog can show you that every person has a unique scent. Although humans have come to rely more on vision, we may still have unconscious reactions to a person's scent. A woman's sensitivity to the aroma of male musk is most intense just before ovulation. When women live in close contact their menstrual periods tend to lock into synchronism. This appears to result from an unconscious reaction to sweat. In one experiment all direct contact was eliminated other than putting a daily dab of another woman's sweat under the subject's nostrils. Within 3 months, the women's periods fell into synchronism with those of the sweat donor.[8]

If the smell-producing pheromone released from the vagina of an ovulating woman is smeared on a virgin female rhesus monkey, it will turn on male monkeys who normally ignore females who are not in heat.[9] Another researcher found a strong tendency for a husband's blood testosterone level to peak 7 days after his wife's ovulation. This is in synchronism with the wife's postovulatory peak in testosterone.[10] These unconscious responses to scent prove that behavior can be affected by smells that we don't even notice.

BODY LANGUAGE

Another major unconscious component in our response to the opposite sex is our body language. When we interact with another person, the eyes also converse in their own way, without our knowing. Our pupils, unconsciously, dilate with pleasure. Researchers have shown that this happens when we look at a sexy picture or a luscious plate of food. One experimenter[11] carefully retouched pictures of pretty women so that each woman was represented twice: once retouched with large pupils, and the other with small pupils. He then showed the pictures to a group of men and asked them what they imagined the women's personalities to be. The faces with enlarged pupils were rated "soft," "pretty," and "feminine," while the small pupil versions were thought to be "hard," "selfish," and "cold." Without knowing, the men were reacting to the unconscious signaling system of the eyes.

When a man and a woman look at each other, "good chemistry" is signaled by dilation of the pupils in a positive feedback: The warmth felt from one person's dilation causes an answering response from the other. Another important signal, when strangers meet, is the length of holding their gaze. Holding the gaze a little longer than the polite time limit is an amazingly strong signal. Holding the gaze and then glancing quickly at the genitals and back to the eyes is an invitation that one can feel without actually noticing it. Eye movement studies show this as a normal response that most of us do without realizing it. Standing closer than the normal distance for strangers can produce a feeling of "magic" even if it isn't consciously noticed. The subtle signals of body language are often in complete disagreement with what we say verbally.

Dr. Fritz Perls of California's Esalen Institute has developed a kind of Gestalt therapy[12] based on carefully watching body language, facial expression, and tone of voice during conversation. These nonverbal channels may be controlled by a different module than the one that wins control of the vocal apparatus. The therapist watches these clues and points out obvious conflicts between what the patients say and what they really feel as indicated by body language, tone of voice, pauses, and other subtle clues. Since the self module is often out of touch with our real feelings and motivations, monitoring these more primitive communication channels can often give a better understanding of our true feelings. Dr. Perls believes that repression affects only the *words* we say, not the other, less conscious, forms of communication such as voice inflection and body language.

The old pop song lyric, "If you want to know if he loves you so, it's in his kiss," has it right. Touching is another primitive form of communication that betrays our true feelings. In the form of hugging, cuddling, and kissing, touch is a much more direct communication of true feelings than are words, which can, in fact, be in direct conflict with actual feelings. Many love relationships demonstrate the dissociation some people have between feelings and logic. A love relationship is really two separate relationships: one verbal and the other nonverbal. It is not uncommon for one to be good, while the other is bad. If your self module is out of touch with your feelings, you can turn the joy of love into an exercise in frustration. Logical theories about love or about your ideal mate should not totally override your equally important, nonverbal feelings. The chart below illustrates the two modes of experiencing a lover:

Logical-verbal attributes	Nonverbal attributes
smart	warm
rich	sexy
eligible	smells good
sensible	feels good
lives nearby	sensitive
	looks good

THE CONCEPT OF LOVE

Evolution has given us a brain built up in layers, with the verbal and logical parts added last. Although the self module tries to speak for all levels of the brain, it is often mistaken—particularly in matters of love. The verbal concept of love often includes the false belief that our self module can explain our primitive feelings. It can override and profoundly affect the quality of those feelings. Though the concept of love varies greatly between cultures, a recent cross-cultural study of romantic love in 168 different cultures by W. R. Jankowiak and E. F. Fischer[13] found that 87% had some concept of romantic love. The researchers felt that the anthropologists whose reports they tabulated may not have asked the question correctly in the cultures where no romance was reported. Clearly, there is a biological basis for love, but the pleasure and pain it can produce are strongly affected by one's belief system.

In our culture, love and marriage are equated. However, in most parts of the world a wife is considered an addition to the extended family rather than an individual object of love. In those cultures love is often a thing that occurs outside of marriage. Love in Samoa,[14] for example, is quite romantic, including ardent love songs and love letters, but not monogamy. Their philosophy is that one love will quickly cure another.

The extended family provides a stable setting where husband and wife need not have the closeness demanded by our nuclear family. Our society has raised the expectations of married life, while at the same time narrowing self boundaries to such an extent that many people are so self-contained they find it impossible to extend their self boundary to include a mate.

The Western concept of love that lasts forever is supported only for the first few years by instinctive bonding. Though mutual bonding with children can provide a basis for a longer-term bond, a duration of 3 years or so makes evolutionary sense as a period when fatherly support is most necessary to ensure infant survival. The most common time couples divorce, in most Western countries, is after about 4 years of marriage.[15]

The concept of love and marriage varies considerably in the different cultures of the world. For example, our disapproval of premarital and extramarital sex is shared by only 10 of 190 non-Western societies covered by one study.[16]

LOVE AND THE LIBERATED WOMAN

One of the great issues in modern American love is the changed role of women. Most of us have intellectually rethought the traditional idea of merged self where the woman is expected to surrender her self and become a mere extension of the man. The residual effects of the old concept make it very difficult to achieve the ideal of an equal merging of selves, with each partner preserving an intact individual self. Ideally, both partners should be open to expanding their world to include some of the interests and insights of their partner. Some modern women feel threatened by this interaction because they lack confidence that their self will survive. As a result, they erect a wall that makes real partnership impossible. Some men still make this fear real by failing to understand that growth must be equal, in both directions.

A true merging of selves means there is no competition. Any accomplishment becomes a joint achievement, which bolsters the sense of pride of both parties. When two secure selves merge there is no need for defensiveness. A poorly defined self, entering into a relationship, may easily be engulfed because the person's need to be merged comes from weakness. Unfortunately, the development of a secure self is a lifetime task influenced strongly by childhood family interactions. Teenagers who are unable to forge an independent self often resort to negative behavior that brings their boundaries up against parents, teachers, or police. These behavior strategies can be carried into adulthood, wreaking havoc with relationships.

Behavior patterns developed in childhood and early adulthood are firmly and separately ingrained in many modules other than the self module. When we change our beliefs by reading books, discussing issues, and even psychotherapy, we are mainly changing concepts in the self module. Conflicting behavior and feelings often remain, but the self module tries to rationalize them to fit its new beliefs. The result can be quite obvious to other people, but the self, believing that it controls all behavior, is furious at the suggestion that old-fashioned values are still showing through.

One common example of this is in open sexual relationships: An intellectual decision by the self module to allow your mate to date others is fine in theory until it actually happens. The negative emotions from other, less enlightened, modules are rationalized by the self. The self module misidentifies the source of the anger into something acceptable under the new sexually liberated belief system. Trying frantically to act as press secretary for the other modules, the self module will come up with amazingly convoluted logic to explain the anger. Some small infraction of manners may be given as the explanation for a major fight or breakup that is actually the result of old-fashioned feelings of jealousy. The negative emotions are there for reasons unknown to the self module, but the behavior must be explained within the framework of the current liberated beliefs of the self.

Anytime you change your beliefs you must be aware that there are other less intellectual modules that are left behind and are still conditioned to feel and behave in the old way. If your self module can accept the fact that other modules, which have not yet changed, may have been in control of behavior, you can avoid the trap of misinterpreting your own behavior. Ideally your self module can at least learn to know your other modules. Changing them is another matter.

THE LOVE MODULE

Our basic gut-level response to love is controlled by a mental module that was formed when we first responded to the loving interaction with our mother in the first months of life. As we mature, this module evolves and is molded by witnessing our parents' loving interactions and then by love experiences with the opposite sex. This module controls our behavior during warm moments with a lover such as cuddling, lovemaking, or watching a sunset together.

Our self module tries to interpret these moments using logical beliefs we have learned. It may elect to interfere with these moments by refusing to yield control to what it perceives as our weak and vulnerable side. Our concept of love can easily spoil the moment if the self module feels it must defend itself. Survival is the rule for anything produced by evolution; our self module will fight with a vengeance against all perceived threats. Giving in to love means opening the boundaries of self to include another. If our self module is insecure, it will panic at the threat of being open to domination or hurt.

Loving requires the trust and confidence of a self module that is willing to release its grip on the controls. A common destructive pattern is when the insecure self module gives in to love, for a while, and then grabs the controls in panic by creating a conflict that will undo the perceived threat. Once a fight is under way, the self module again loses control to another specialist module that has evolved from the crying and negative behavior module formed in infancy. This *fight module* incorporates many patterns from your childhood experiences with your parents' fighting behavior. After your fight module has been in control you may honestly say, "I wasn't myself," because your self module can only guess why you behaved as you did.

When you exercise self-control to avoid a fight, you don't allow the fight module to take control. While this seems like a good idea, it may make matters worse in the long run because the feelings of the fight module go unexpressed and may build up to become a destructive force. The better solution is to develop a healthy fight module that can safely be allowed to take control by intentionally releasing self-control on minor disputes. The fight module is thus able to express itself *before* its frustration builds to a breaking point. Disputes are thus settled before they become ugly. Again, the principle is for the self module to stand aside and allow the specialist modules to do their job and develop in a healthy way.

If we translate this into a healthy concept of love, it means accepting the idea of respectful but possibly somewhat heated disputes with the one you love. It also means giving in freely to the passion of love with a mutual understanding that you will each respect the unique self of the other while opening up your own self boundary. This may be the hardest part because it involves trusting your mate not to take advantage of your openness. If you have had bad experiences or if your parents set a bad example, this can be difficult. You can easily become stuck in the positive feedback of a false belief, which will make it look convincingly like nobody can be trusted. This false belief will make you sense that a person, who really can be trusted, is up to something. It is easy to become locked into a pattern of suspicion that no mortal can break through. Of course, the opposite situation is also possible; if you believe that everyone can be trusted, then you will ignore clear signs of dishonesty and fall in love with people who will hurt you. As with all false beliefs, there is no easy solution. You must continually reexamine your beliefs with the realization that your present beliefs may be falsely confirmed by your distorted perception. When in doubt, it is usually better to err on the positive side.

SENSUOUS LOVE

A love relationship is a perfect opportunity to make a mutual pact to develop your nonverbal modules together. Your relationship with a lover has many separate aspects that should all act harmoniously together.

Your sense of smell, for example, forms the basis of an interaction at the most basic instinctual level. It is probably not based on a module at the level of the self module but rather on instinctive structures[17] deep in the reptilian part of your brain. Regardless of the exact location, the important thing is that your self module must learn to stand back at times and allow the unfettered richness of your direct interaction with your lover's smell. Soaps and colognes can be enjoyable in themselves but they tend to mask the unique individual smell of the person. Watch the way a dog interacts with and loves its master's smell. If you practice the same kind of interaction with your lover you may be able to uncover a whole new dimension to your relationship. In a famous letter, Napoleon asked Josephine[18] not to bathe for two weeks before they were to reunite. The French poet Baudelaire[19] wrote, "My soul soars upon your perfume as other mens souls soar upon music." Our society has taught us to deny such feelings. You can work with your lover to free yourselves from this loss: Both of you agree to close your eyes and focus on using smell and taste only to explore each other.

Each of your senses has its own way of contributing to an intimate love relationship. You use your hearing when you talk to your lover but there is a more primitive kind of vocal communications that reaches deeper areas of the brain. Sighs and moans during lovemaking and affectionate embraces come from other parts of the brain. This is a perfect example of how control of the speech apparatus is assigned to one module only. If you are talking while making love, the sighs and moans stop because they originate in a more primitive part of your brain that is controlling your body movements but is overpowered for vocal control by the module doing the talking. When the talking stops, the speech apparatus is again available for sensuous control.

Control goes to the module that has been most reinforced in this context; unfortunately that is not necessarily the best-qualified module. Often we miss out on sensuous experience because the self module has a bad habit of taking over at inappropriate times. With practice these habits can be changed. Make a pact with your lover against talking during lovemaking and focus instead on communicating with more primitive sensuous sounds.

Touching is another primitive form of communication that can best be practiced with a lover. Close your eyes or wear a blindfold while you focus on just one sense at a time. By learning to respect and support these more primitive forms of communications you can gradually undo the tyranny of an overdeveloped self module. While self-control is extremely important during some aspects of your life, it can rob life of its joy and meaning at other times. The important thing is to develop a balance and flexibility in your thinking that allows each specialist to develop fully and gain control at the appropriate time.

CHAPTER TWELVE

The Empty Self

To live is like to love—all reason is against it,
and all healthy instinct for it.
—— *Samuel Butler, 1902*

Reason is, and ought to be, the slave of the passions.
—— *David Hume, 1739*

Emotion is the chief source of all becoming-consciousness.
There can be no transforming of darkness into light
and of apathy into movement without emotion.
—— *Carl Jung, 1938*

Every culture has a prevailing self-concept that strongly affects its citizens' potential for progress and happiness. In Chapter Five we saw how a change in self-concept made an explosion of creativity and progress possible in Renaissance Europe. In the recent past the American self-concept has undergone significant changes that may be the cause of many social problems, such as crime, teen suicide,[1] and drug abuse. The ideal of an autonomous, bounded, masterful self has reached an extreme that Philip Cushman has called the *empty self*.

Throughout this century the boundaries of self have undergone continual shrinkage. The extended family, which was common before the turn of the century, has all but disappeared. Older people, who used to remain an important part of the family, are now institutionalized. The percentage of American households of seven or more persons declined from 35.9% in 1790 to 20.4% in 1900 to 5.8% in 1950. Even the nuclear family seems to be endangered as more and more people choose to live alone. Divorced and unwed mothers are often choosing to live alone with their children. The number of single-parent households has tripled since 1960. One-third of all children today are raised in a household with only one or no parents present; in the black community the figure is two-thirds. Households consisting of only one person rose from 3.7% in 1790 to 9.3% in 1950 to 18.5% in 1973.[2] Privacy has become an obsession. Fences isolate backyards in many areas, and front porches, formerly places to chat with your neighbors out for a walk, have been enclosed or abandoned. Parties and socializing with neighbors and friends have become a thing of the past for some people as they draw in their self boundaries and follow the new trend of "cocooning." The continuing trend is toward narrowing the boundaries of self to their ultimate limit—the private, self-contained individual cut off from all attachments to family, community, and traditions.

FILLING THE VOID

The void created by this loss of a shared tribal or community identity is often filled in in modern society by identifying with professional sports teams and superstar public celebrities. Advertising has become less focused on the product itself and more on an identification with a superstar or lifestyle image. Designer names on clothes are more important than their actual style or quality. Often, the designer name itself is a highly visible part of the design so that people will be certain to notice.

Identification with professional sports teams provides a needed extension to the self that replaces the tribal identity. If the home team wins, fans are heard to yell "*We* won!" and "*We* are the best!" even though most of the players are not even from the city identified with the team. Teenage gangs are on the increase because they provide an extension of the self and an identity that fills the void left by the collapse of both the nuclear and the extended family. The self-improvement industry is thriving with workshops on such things as channeling, which puts your self in touch with a spirit guide who is attached to you for life. Products for losing weight, firming up, and eliminating wrinkles fight for advertising space. One cable channel sells nothing but exercise machines and self-improvement products. We even have a popular magazine called *Self*. Overeating and drug abuse may just be attempts to fill the empty self. Shopaholics try to fill their emptiness by filling their closets.

NEW CONCEPTS OF CONTROL

The concept of the self-contained individual has destroyed the network of group loyalties and connections between people that used to keep society and business together. In the United States, the legal profession has encouraged this mentality and mushroomed to fill the gap. Instead of interactions based on common sense and goodwill between connected people, we have legalized our dealings with one another. The United States has *30 times more lawsuits per person and* 20 *times as many lawyers per person as Japan.*[3]

One of the consequences of this new lawsuit fever is the victim mentality. Exactly the opposite of the concept of the self-in-control, victims feel helpless to control their own life. Instead of taking personal responsibility for their misfortunes, the modern tendency is to always search for an *external* cause: If we spill hot coffee on our lap or slip on the sidewalk, the modern trend is to sue the restaurant rather than take personal responsibility.

If we can identify with a group of victims we can excuse all of our failures because a "conspiracy" makes success impossible. Instead of being the object of scorn we can become the object of pity. The conspiracy can be corporate, male, white, black, big business, parents, or any other identifiable group. Lawyers have benefitted greatly from this concept because lawsuits are the main defense against conspiracies. The problem is that the victim often takes no personal responsibility for his or her own actions, focusing instead on the evil of the victimizer. Instead of working on the problem by trying harder to gain respect, the victim declares war and actually makes the problem worse.

By banding together in special groups, victims gain a group identity that supports them in their fight against the enemy. In such groups victim-oriented beliefs are implanted and reinforced by the group, adding more positive feedback to that already built into the victim's mind. The victim's belief causes him to see confirming evidence of the conspiracy everywhere.

The sense of belonging to a group with a common identity fills the void that used to be filled by family, community, and job loyalty. Some of the militant black, racist white, gay, and women's and men's rights victim-oriented groups work themselves into such a hostile frenzy that any successful contact with the enemy is perceived as a betrayal of the cause. Efforts toward reconciliation are tantamount to treason.[4]

Child abuse and dysfunctional family life has been found to be a common factor in the background of many criminals. Unfortunately, the useful and necessary discussion of this fact in the press is picked up by people looking for an easy way out. By incorporating the abuse victim belief into their self-concept they feel free to break the law and be pitied for it. A new trend is to use the abuse excuse in court to defend murderers and thieves. The victim label allows them to escape responsibility for crimes that they actually committed out of greed, malice, or laziness. Victim labels are attractive because they give people permission to escape from the hard realities of life and receive pity instead of condemnation for their actions.

While some people have given up on the concept of any control of their own lives, there are other popular movements that have taken the concept of self-in-control to the other extreme—where control of reality is absolute. A popular bumper sticker a few years ago was "Visualize World Peace." Surely this must be the ultimate extension of the concept of the self-in-control. Under this self-concept, the complex external world of politics becomes a part of, and controllable by, the individual. Another variation of this concept promises that *anyone* can become anything they want to if they just try hard enough. This extreme of the self-concept in *complete* control without limitations can cause as much unhappiness and disappointment as the opposite extreme. While free will is a powerful concept that can allow us to take control of our lives and overcome incredible difficulties, it cannot stop a bullet hurtling toward us. An important part of a healthy self-concept is an understanding of which apparent limitations are real.

THE MEANING IN LIFE

Science and logic have brought our knowledge to a point that we now see ourselves, not as the center of the universe, but as insignificant grains of sand in a small solar system destined to explode into a supernova someday. This depressing view of life is found in countless works of literature and philosophy. Of all of the animals, only man can talk himself into such a state of despair that he commits suicide.

Life is absurd, the existentialists say. This sentiment is the inevitable result of trying to apply logic to an inappropriate problem. While the logical, objective point of view has accomplished marvelous things in the field of science, it is *not* appropriate for finding meaning in life. Animals have no problem with meaning, nor will we if we can just listen to the older and wiser parts of our brain. It doesn't matter if life in general has an *objective* meaning; what matters is the subjective meaning in *our* life. Life has meaning, not *of* it but *in* it.[5]

People in love never feel that life is absurd. The question never comes up because they are too busy *feeling* the joy of life. Our basic drives and emotions give life a meaning and a purpose if we allow them. One of the flaws in the modern self-concept is an overemphasis on self-control that often stifles our less logical emotional side. The modern logical self module often sees emotions as troublesome and misleading distortions. In reality they are often the very things that give life meaning.

Emotions have their own logic. Instead of being subdued, they should be respected and nurtured to health by the self. The specialized modules of the mind all have their own area of competence. The self, with its cold logic, is the least qualified to find meaning in life and must learn to yield that task to more qualified modules. The ultimate demonstration of the harm done by our culture's worship of the self may be when people commit suicide because they can find no meaning in life. Truly this is the self module run amuck.

RELEARNING YOUR REALITY

We have all had a lifetime of practice viewing reality through a false belief system that ignores all but one of the specialized modules of our mind. The tyranny of the self module's takeover of reality is not easily overthrown. We must use our knowledge of the actual organization of the brain to gradually relearn how to correctly interpret our own reality. With practice we can learn to recognize the difference between the real introspection of verbal thoughts within the self module and the imaginative filling-in we use to maintain our false belief in a singular mind.

We should be thankful for our brain's very useful ability to fill-in gaps to make sense of the world. However, we must also be extremely cautious of the false sense of certainty it provides. False beliefs are confirmed so convincingly that seeing the truth can be extremely difficult. The blind spot in your vision is a handy reminder of just how difficult it can be to see objective reality. Without a special demonstration like the one on page 38, you would swear that it doesn't exist. Other false beliefs are equally hard to see through. Wherever there is hate and strife you will find opposing belief systems that are convincingly confirmed for each side. Learning to see past these false confirmations in your own life takes effort and practice.

FIGURE 11. A happy team of specialist modules works together, each doing what it does best.

It also takes practice to change your self module from a tyrant to a nurturing and supportive parent. You will be amazed at what you can accomplish when you become aware of the team of specialists you are blessed with. With time and effort you can develop this family of modules into a happy team where each member gets the opportunity to develop its own unique qualities to full potential.

APPENDIX ONE

The Cognitive Revolution

In 1981 Dr. Roger Sperry of Caltech won a Nobel Prize for his pioneering work on understanding the organization of the brain. Since it was Sperry's work that led to the insights we have been exploring in this book, a review of his fascinating split-brain experiments is in order.

The brains of all mammals are divided into two distinctly separate halves, or hemispheres, which are connected only by a narrow band of nerves called the corpus callosum. Each half of the brain is directly connected only to the nerves and muscles on the *opposite* side of the body. The optic nerve connections to the retina of the eye are likewise crossed so that the right half of the brain sees only the left side of the visual field[1] and vice versa. This separation of control has a survival value because during a battle you have two independent channels at work: Threats from the right can be dealt with by the left brain while at the same time the right brain handles threats from the left.

THE SPLIT-BRAIN EXPERIMENTS

Back in the 1950s, Dr. Sperry began doing animal experiments to discover how the two halves of the brain interact. These experiments ultimately led to his being awarded the Nobel prize. He found that when the two hemispheres of a cat's or monkey's brain were surgically separated, the animals remained remarkably normal. Sperry created an apparatus for separately communicating with each half of the animal's brain by briefly flashing images to their left or right visual field. The animal was trained to use one paw or the other to press a lever in response to specific flashed shapes. Since the left visual field and the left paw are controlled by the right hemisphere, and vice versa, he was able to demonstrate *separate and independent learning in the two halves of the animal's brain.* He separately trained each side of the animal for a different response: The right paw (left hemisphere) was trained to press a lever whenever an "X" was flashed on the right, but ignore an "O"; the left side was trained to do the exact opposite. It was almost as if the animal had two separate minds, each trained for a different response.

The real breakthrough came in 1962 when Dr. Sperry, and his students Michael Gazzaniga and Jerre Levy, had the opportunity to study a *human* split-brain patient who had undergone the split-brain surgery to control epileptic seizures. Though the split-brain surgery had been done on other humans 20 years earlier and the examining doctors had concluded that the operation had no effect on the patients' mental abilities, Sperry used his new test techniques to separately test the two halves of the new patient's brain with amazing results.

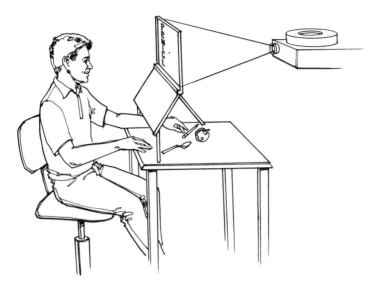

FIGURE 12. A classic split-brain experiment of Sperry. The subject stares at a spot on the screen while a slide projector flashes a message to the nonverbal side of the subject's surgically split brain. In the example shown he will be verbally unaware that he saw the word "pencil" yet his left hand will easily retrieve the pencil from the selection of objects.

The apparatus used is illustrated in Figure 12. Information was communicated to only one side of the subject's brain at a time by having him stare at a spot while words or pictures were flashed to one side or the other of his visual field. By having the subject respond with one hand or the other, it was possible to get separate responses from each hemisphere. For example, when the word "pencil" was flashed on the left, the subject's left hand could easily pick a pencil out of a collection of objects hidden behind a panel. His right hand couldn't pick the correct object because that side of the brain only saw things on the right and had therefore seen nothing. Since normal communications between the two halves of the brain were cut, each hand could respond only if the message was flashed on its side of vision.

The amazing part was when the subject was asked which object he had picked *he could answer only for his right hand*. When his left hand picked something he would insist that he had seen nothing! When pressed for an explanation, he would answer something like, "Well, I must have done it unconsciously," or "I guessed."[2] Clearly his self module only knew about the messages flashed on the right side. The actual act of reading the flashed message and picking an object on the left was clearly done by an independent module on the other side of his brain!

Without the unifying control of the connections between the two halves of the brain, the patient sometimes had conflicts that clearly demonstrated the separate parallel modules of the mind. To quote an article by Sperry[3]:

> . . . while the patient was dressing and trying to pull on his trousers the left hand might start to work against the right to pull the trousers down on that side. Or, the left hand, after just helping to tie the belt of the patient's robe, might go ahead on its own to untie the completed knot, whereupon the right hand would have to supervene again to retie it. The patient and his wife used to refer to the "sinister left hand" that sometimes tried to push the wife away aggressively at the same time that the hemisphere of the right hand was trying to get her to come and help him with something.

Such conflicts are not common because the two halves of the brain normally develop a kind of working agreement whereby each side tends to take over control in situations where it feels most comfortable. In another article[4] Dr. Sperry summarized the effect of the operation as follows:

> . . . in the split brain syndrome we deal with two separate spheres of conscious awareness, i.e., two separate conscious entities or minds running in parallel in the same cranium, each with its own sensations, perceptions, cognitive processes, learning experiences, memories, and so on.

Though it didn't become clear until many years later, this demonstration of two centers of thinking in one head was only a beginning. The simplified concept of two kinds of thinking was a useful first step that was easily demonstrated in the split-brain patients. Later studies, by Dr. Michael Gazzaniga, on dozens of other patients who had undergone the split-brain operation convinced him that the mind was actually divided into a large number of separate modules. One of these modules, which he called the "interpreter," tried to explain all behavior, even when that behavior was clearly driven by other modules. For example, in one experiment Gazzaniga flashed the word "laugh" to the subject's right, nonverbal, hemisphere. To quote Gazzaniga[5]:

> After the stimulus was presented, one patient laughed and, when asked why, said: "you guys come up and test us every month. What a way to make a living!" In still another example, when the command "walk" is flashed to the right hemisphere, patients will typically stand up from their chairs and begin to leave the testing van. When asked where he or she is

going, the person's left brain says, for example, "I'm going into the house to get a coke." However you manipulate this type of test, it always yields the same kind of result.

The split-brain patients make it possible to scientifically demonstrate the firmly ingrained habit the self module has of making up stories to explain and take credit for behavior caused by other modules. Since the right brain modules are surgically disconnected, we know positively when the behavior was not under control of the self. Since the self module can be very clever at using subtle cues, the split-brain patients can appear very normal if special apparatus is not used. For example, without the special flash projection apparatus, eye movements make it possible for both hemispheres to see both sides of vision.

If the hands are not obscured from vision during left-hand pointing responses, the self module can see what the left hand pointed to and will, without hesitation, use this information to explain the response. For example, in one experiment a snow scene was flashed on the left and a chicken claw on the right. The subject pointed with his right hand at a card on the table with a chicken on it, and his left hand chose a snow shovel. When asked why he made these choices he answered, without hesitation, "Oh, that's easy. The chicken claw goes with the chicken and you need a shovel to clean out the chicken shed."[6] A normal person would have known that the shovel was a snow shovel but, deprived of the stronger answer that seeing the snow scene would have provided, the subject's self module simply confabulated a plausible answer.

Without the special lab setup, the split-brain patients are so good at bluffing their way around their handicaps that they appear quite normal to most observers. Back in the 1940s, Dr. A. J. Akelaitis performed split-brain surgery on 25 patients. His published report concluded that the operation had *no effect* on the patients' mental or physical abilities.[7] The self module's long standing habit of "filling in" to fabricate a consistent conscious experience makes disconnection of half of the brain an event that is scarcely noticed.

Extensive testing of the separate abilities of the left and right hemispheres of the brain has uncovered a consistent pattern: One side of the brain, the left for 95% of the population, specializes in language and logic but has poor spatial and emotional capabilities. The other hemisphere has poor language and logical abilities but is good at spatial, emotional, and other nonverbal tasks. This specialization is not surprising when you consider the process of spontaneous organization under which mental modules form: The first glimmering of speech ability on one side of the brain tends to give an advantage to neurons in the same vicinity for any new module formation that involves language or logic. On nonverbal tasks, the other side of the brain gains an advantage as nonverbal modules form in a sort of specialized community. For the 5% of the population where speech happens to organize in the right hemisphere, the roles of the hemispheres are simply reversed. Each person develops a unique brain organization, working around inevitable defects in the neuron network. Some people develop considerable speech on both sides of their brain, and, in fact, women tend to have more verbal abilities in both hemispheres[8] than men.

It has been well known for centuries that women have a better prognosis for recovery after strokes that damage speech abilities. This is the result of a significant difference in the degree of specialization between the two hemispheres of the brain. Because the neural connections between hemispheres are not completely developed in infancy, during early development the infant is almost like a split-brain patient.[9] Modules spontaneously organize in the separate halves of the brain with very little cooperation or interaction possible until about the age of six, when development (myelination) of these connections is completed. Since girls mature significantly faster than boys,[10] cooperation and interaction between the two halves of the brain become possible earlier in development. This results in less specialization between left and right brain organization and more language abilities in the nonverbal hemisphere. Given the extreme sensitivity of the spontaneous organization process, this earlier joining of the two hemispheres in girls could be an important explanation for the differing brain organizations of men and women.

THE COGNITIVE REVOLUTION

The concepts we have been discussing represent but one aspect of revolution that has now spread from psychology to numerous other fields of science. The successful overthrow of behaviorism and incorporation of consciousness into our model of the mind required a revolutionary new scientific paradigm that has grown in popularity in recent years. For centuries science has focused on the principle of *microdeterminism*, i.e., the idea that if you study the tiny, solvable, details an overall understanding of the whole system will follow. In recent years, it has become clear that this approach will not work with many real-world problems: *The whole is often much more than the sum of its parts*, and most important emergent properties in nature are not at all predictable by studying the basic components.

For example, though water is simply a combination of hydrogen and oxygen atoms, studying the characteristics of these atoms gives us no hint of what the marvelous properties of water will be. Likewise, studying an individual bee gives us no inkling of the complex properties that will emerge when bees assemble together in a colony. The miracle of human intelligence and consciousness that emerges from a relatively random assemblage of neurons would never be predicted by studying those neurons in isolation.

Behaviorism was an attempt to make psychology "scientific" by objectively studying the basic stimulus–response elements of behavior. Consciousness and introspection were completely rejected as factors because they appeared to be so unreliable. Between 1915 and 1965, behaviorism was the dominant school of psychology in the United States. It failed to produce useful results because consciousness cannot be ignored and the emergent properties of the mind are simply not predictable from reductionist models. Though introspection is inaccurate fantasy when applied to all but the self module, it is nonetheless important because it often affects our behavior since we *think* it is accurate. Consciousness is often not in control, but it can and does drive our behavior at some very crucial times.

The cognitive revolution was finally able to displace behaviorism in the 1970s because a new paradigm was developed that allowed a top-down approach to systems analysis to be superimposed on the traditional bottom-up reductionist approach. Studying the emergent characteristics of a colony of bees helps us explain and predict the movements of the individual bees as they follow their evolved group behavior patterns. Without this kind of analysis, the behavior of an individual bee makes no sense at all and is unpredictable. Dr. Sperry calls this the principle of *downward causation*.[11] Applied to the mind, it means that, *if you want to explain and predict neuron firings, you must consider the thoughts of the mind that emerge from those neurons*. All of the traditional, upward-acting scientific principles continue to apply and be useful, but the downward causation principle is superimposed, allowing us to develop a deeper understanding.

In psychology this means that much of the work of the behaviorists is still valid and useful but that their mistake was in completely rejecting the effect of consciousness. Since introspection is done by the self module it is accurate only for the thoughts of the self module. Though the self module is often not in control, it can and does take control at crucial times. Self-control and consciousness cannot be ignored.

After centuries of attempts to understand the human mind, it is amazing that our basic understanding is still so crude that many people in the field still speak of the mind as a singular entity. Paradigm changes take time to be absorbed. Perhaps with this new knowledge we can finally begin to truly understand the human mind.

APPENDIX TWO

A Summary of Conclusions

1. The neurons of the brain spontaneously organize into hundreds of separate, specialized modules.

2. At any given moment the one module that has been most reinforced in the current context takes control of our speech.

3. A similar control-to-the-strongest mechanism allows only one module to control body movement at any given moment. This may or may not be the same module that controls speech.

4. All modules can monitor the inputs from the senses at all times, though some do not because some sense inputs are not relevant to their specialty.

5. Some modules produce an experience of consciousness, but in modern Western culture, one module, which we call the self, tends to hog the spotlight and make us ignore other kinds of consciousness.

6. The self module is a specialist at calm, logical, verbal behavior. It is engaged when we do introspection.

7. The self module uses concepts, learned in childhood, to construct an imaginary, unified world fulfilling our expectations.

8. The brain is good at filling in to make sense of the world by perceiving it in a way that fits expectations.

9. The learned expectations of the self module are called beliefs.

10. Introspection and consciousness distort perception to make it fit these beliefs. Initial beliefs thus tend to be confirmed and strengthened by experience—even if they are false.

11. Most of our behavior is not controlled by the self module. However, the modern Western self-concept includes beliefs that the self module is able to introspect and explain all behavior.

12. The self module attempts to explain our behavior, which it observed but didn't control, by constructing a system of beliefs deduced from our own observed behavior.

13. Though introspection is usually nothing more than imaginative theorizing based on past observations, after a lifetime of practice it begins to feel like direct, private knowledge of our mental processes.

14. The only introspection that is not imagined is when we look at the self module itself: self-controlled behavior such as step-by-step logical

thinking, long-term planning, and goal-oriented overriding of instinctive behavior.

15. Memory recall is a creative process that includes distortion to make it fit our beliefs and strengthen our self-esteem. Memories can be created and altered by later events.

16. Our sense of time is also creatively distorted to make perception fit our expectations.

17. Nonverbal, emotional behavior has its own logic, which is more effective than verbal logic in many situations. It brings meaning to life.

18. Self-control should be used with caution because it may stifle the development of a module better qualified for the job at hand.

19. The modern Western self module suffers from the false belief that it is the center of all consciousness and all reliable thinking.

Notes

CHAPTER ONE: THE
SELF-ORGANIZING MIND

1. Software is the changeable part of a computer that determines what it will actually do. It is usually purchased on a diskette and updated regularly with improved versions. One of the reasons computer technology has evolved so rapidly is that the physical hardware of the computer can remain the same while the functionality can be improved by loading in new software programs. The brain has also remained fixed through recorded history, but human capabilities can change quickly when learned concepts change. The self-concepts are similar to the operating system on a computer in that they define the basic reality under which other learning and perception will operate.

2. See Appendix One for more details on Sperry's split-brain experiments.

3. Chaos theory mathematically addresses extremely complicated problems such as global weather and self-organizing natural formations (see Gleik, 1987). Complexity theory focuses on the edge of chaos. It has yet to mature into a real science, but people are hard at work trying to generalize its principles. A think-tank organization has been formed in Santa Fe, New Mexico (see Waldrop, 1992, and Kauffman, 1991). Both sciences are trying to generalize the principles of self-organization.

4. I will use the term *spontaneous organization* sometimes in place of the more conventional *self-organization* because it more accurately describes the process in which organization occurs spontaneously as a result of the characteristics of the individual entities—without any central control or coordination. For more on self-organization see Prigogine and Stenses (1984) and also Koestler (1967).

5. Cell-building is normally done after graduating from feeding young larva at an age of about 10 days. At 20 days of age the bee is ready to begin guard duty at the entrance to the hive. Eventually, foraging for food becomes the bee's lifetime occupation (Koestler, 1967, p. 107).

6. We actually have another separate immune system that protects infants before this antibody system is fully functional. It is probably a remnant of earlier evolution that remains active to fill the gap before the newer immune system is ready to become active.

7. He also called it the theory of neuronal group selection (see Edelman, 1985, 1992).

8. See Waldrop (1992, p. 158).

9. See Waldrop (1992, p. 191).

10. PET stands for positron emission tomography. It actually produces detailed three-dimensional views of the brain metabolism increases that occur in active parts of the brain. Water with a radioactive marker is injected in a vein in the arm, and the positrons released as it decays produce radiation. Computerized analysis then reconstructs a plot of activity. The plots in the figure are obtained by calculating the difference in activity between a rest state and during the mental task (Raichle, 1994).

11. Credit must be given to Michael Gazzaniga for developing the idea of a separate verbal "interpreter" module in the left brain. He developed this concept after decades of working with split-brain patients who often make up elaborate verbal explanations for behavior known to be caused by the surgically disconnected right hemisphere of their brain (Gazzaniga, 1985).

12. Quoted in Tart (1975, p. 164).

13. See Dennett (1991, p. 215).

CHAPTER TWO: GETTING TO KNOW YOUR SELF MODULE

1. The degree of awareness of an internal verbal dialogue certainly varies greatly between individuals. Some people talk aloud to themselves or make subtle movements of their speech apparatus; others are probably aware of very few internal words. These remarks reflect the author's experience of consciousness, but the principles are hopefully fairly general.

2. See Blakeslee (1980, pp. 152–155).

3. Because the demonstration of gap filling in Figure 2 is a very important one to the rest of the book, make sure you see it. If your left eye doesn't see well, turn the book upside down and use your right.

4. Dennett (1992, p. 34).

5. Eye movements plotted with special optical sensing equipment. These eye motions generally occur at a rate of about three to five movements per second, even when we think our eyes are still (Kosslyn and Koenig, 1992, p. 100).

6. Quote from Crick (1994, p. 167).

7. Dennett (1991, p. 361).

8. Cheating experiment demonstrating Festinger's theory of cognitive dissonance (Gazzaniga, 1985, p. 139).

9. In the stockings experiment the bias may have been related to the natural habit of scanning left to right. Since the last stocking was as good as the others, it got chosen as best (Nesbit and Wilson, 1977).

CHAPTER THREE: TIME AND CONSCIOUSNESS

1. Canoe sentence by Lashley (1951) quoted in *Behavioral & Brain Sciences*, 1992, *15*(2), 227 (part of a 55-page discussion of time and the observer).

2. Harth (1992, p. 198).

3. Dennett (1991, p. 197). From a 1963 presentation to the Ostler Society, Oxford University.

4. The electrodes remained in place for a week after surgery. A mild shock was applied to the hand and to an electrode in the neocortex. They each produced a slightly different sensation from a slightly different part of the hand. Even with a 1/4 second delay on the electrode stimulus to the hand, the hand stimulus seemed to occur first. With a 1/2-second delay they seemed simultaneous. The signal seems to go through the thymus, which represses the sensation and then backdates it. *Brain*, 1979, *102*, 193; quoted in Winson (1985, p. 276).

5. Dennett (1991, p. 163).

6. Dennett (1991, p. 325), Crick (1994, pp. 171–172).

7. Restak (1991, pp. 152–153).

8. For an excellent discussion of consciousness, see Jaynes (1976, pp. 1–66). The flashlight analogy is on page 23. For a further discussion of our mind's distortion of time and the illusions of consciousness by a philosopher, see Dennett (1991). Caution: He uses words like "heterophe-nomenological."

CHAPTER FOUR:
MEMORY ILLUSIONS

1. The study showing 60% incidence of confabulation after damage is in Weinstein and Lyerly (1968, p. 250). Another study of denial of symptoms is in Prigatano and Schacter (1991, p. 254).

2. John Dean's memory: A case study, *Cognition*, 1981, *9*, 1–22; quoted in Goleman (1985, p. 93).

3. Piaget quoted in Loftus and Ketcham (1991).

4. Actual measurement of distinct electrical patterns in the parts of the animal brains that distinguish smells has shown that when a new smell is learned, all of the distinct patterns change, indicating that some kind of complete reorganization takes place as new memories are added.

5. Goethals and Reckman (1973). The perception of consistency in attitudes. *Journal of Experimental Psychology,* *9,* 491–501; quoted in Nesbit (1977).

6. Patient J.B.R. couldn't recognize things distinguished primarily by looks (e.g., plants, animals). He had no problem with items distinguished by how you use them (e.g., tools, household objects). V.E.R. had trouble with inanimate objects but no problem identifying food, flowers, or animals. (Kosslyn and Koenig, 1992, p. 229.)

7. See Gazzaniga (1985).

8. Restak (1994, p. 66; p. 68 for categories of memory loss).

CHAPTER FIVE:
OTHER CONCEPTS OF SELF

1. In the world of computer software the self-concept would represent the bottom layer on which specific programs such as your individual personality are added. It is a bit like a computer operating system: a graphical computer interface versus text orientation. Specific programs loaded on top of it will have drastically different characteristics depending on the operating system. Likewise, individual personalities will have drastically different characteristics depending on the underlying self-concept.

2. For a detailed development of the idea of consciousness as a recent invention, see *The Origin of Consciousness in the Breakdown of the Bicameral Mind* by Julian Jaynes (1976), and also Lyons (1978).

3. *Indigenous Psychologies: The Anthropology of the Self,* edited by Heelas and Lock (1981, p. 40).

4. Heelas and Lock (1981, p. 9).

5. Heelas and Lock (1981, p. 545).

6. Quotes from Lee in Jennings (1955, p. 290).

7. Jennings (1955, p. 295).

8. Spanos (1986, p. 461).

9. See Gazzaniga (1988, p. 19).

10. Goodwin Chu quoted in Steinberg and Barnes (1988, p. 276).

11. Princeton anthropologist Clifford Geertz quoted in Gergen (1991, p. 9).

12. Kahn (1973, pp. 7, 103).

13. The brain is divided into two hemispheres, each controlling the opposite half of the body. The responsibility for attending to space on each side seems to be individually assigned, though modules on either side of the brain can normally initiate action on either side. This autonomous control certainly has survival value when things are happening simultaneously on both sides.

14. Jaynes (1976, p. 69; *Iliad* additions, pp. 72–83).

15. Baumeister (1987, p. 165).

16. Taylor (1989, p. 130).

17. Baumeister (1987, p. 169). For more on privacy see Taylor (1989, p. 291).

CHAPTER SIX: FALSE BELIEFS

1. Note that we don't mean positive feedback in the sense of encouragement. Positive feedback in the engineering sense could mean encouragement of someone who already has an optimistic outlook and discouragement of someone who is already discouraged. The positive means that the feedback is in the same direction, as opposed to negative feedback, which would be in the opposite direction. Positive feedback tends to produce instability because a small input will grow as a result of the feedback until some limit is reached.

2. See De Bono (1990, p. 126) for a discussion of circularity.

3. IRA is the Irish Republican Army, a Catholic terrorist group.

4. Goleman (1985, p. 174) discusses "the game of happy family"; see also p. 96 on the self-concept.

5. Goleman (1985, p. 185).

6. Calvin (1991, pp. 111–119) discusses President Wilson's disabilities. For a lengthy discussion of denial after brain injury see Prigatano and Schacter (1991).

7. See Goleman (1985, p. 106). See Figure 3 for a plot of eye movements done with similar equipment.

8. Homeopathy is debunked in Gardner (1957; also Gardner, 1992). For sales growth see *LA Times* 6/13/95, p. E3.

9. Meyers (1992, p. 144).

10. Warwick and Salkovskis (1989, p. 78).

11. Inflation statistics from Congdon (1988, p. 21).

12. Lyons (1988, p. 140).

13. Lyons (1988, p. 139).

14. Pendergrast (1995, p. 360), Lyons (1988, p. 141).

15. See Lyons (1988, pp. 143–145) for brief descriptions of nine of these cases together with a summary of their outcomes.

CHAPTER SEVEN: HYPNOSIS AND OTHER ALTERED STATES

1. Gardner (1992, p. 175).

2. Dianetics is described in one of the best-selling books of all time, *Dianetics* by L. Ron Hubbard. For a discussion see Gardner (1957, p. 269).

3. Spanos *et al.* (1991).

4. Spanos *et al.* (1985, p. 1166).

5. A study by T. R. Sarbin in Jaynes (1976, p. 393).

6. Spanos *et al.* (1985, p. 1165). Also see Fromm (1979).

7. Wynn (1956, p. 78).

8. Spanos *et al.* (1991, p. 310).

9. Experiment in Wynn (1956, p. 130). See also Hilgard (1977). The comments on their conscious experience during hypnosis are reproduced in Spanos *et al.* (1985, p. 1161).

10. Pendergrast (1995).

CHAPTER EIGHT: PSYCHOTHERAPY AND MULTIPLE PERSONALITIES

1. The new official term for MPD according to DSM-IV is Dissociative Identity Disorder.

2. McHugh (1992, p. 507).

3. Barton (1994, p. 169). The case that inspired the book *Sybil* was a classic case of therapy-induced symptoms. Her 16 different personalities were brought out in over 2300 psychotherapy sessions. Another therapist who took her case during the vacations of her main therapist reported that she seemed to be relieved when he allowed her to discuss her problems directly rather than having to "be Peggy" as her normal therapist preferred (Pendergrast, 1995, p. 158).

4. Harold Merskey, Professor Emeritus of Psychiatry at the University of Western Ontario in Canada, reviewed original documents describing cases of MPD before the development of widespread publicity and concluded: "To my surprise, there was not a single case which allowed a valid diagnosis of MPD, free either from a misunderstanding or from the effects of suggestion" (Merskey, 1994, p. 174).

5. Pendergrast (1995, p. 165).

6. Kluft (1993, p. 156). Here is another interesting quote from the same paper: "I will assign pairs or groups of alters the task of talking together about decisions to be made or issues of concern, but most commonly at this stage I want them to do no more than spend time together and hold casual conversations. I want communication channels to be established early on, and for there to be a feeling of fellowship among the alters before I address their areas of discord."

7. Barton (1993, p. 170).

8. Ischlondsky (1955); see also Blakeslee (1980, p. 163–165).

9. Ahern *et al.* (1993).

10. Dissociative Experiences Survey (DES) (Murphy, 1994, p. 29). The DES questionnaire asks you the percent of the time you have each of the following experiences: memory gap when driving a car, gap listening to somebody talk, finding yourself in a place and not knowing how you got there, not knowing how you got dressed in these clothes, finding new things you don't remember buying, meeting strangers who insist they know you, feeling like you are watching yourself, not recognizing friends or family members, no memory of important events in your life, being falsely accused of lying, not recognizing yourself in the mirror, feeling that the world is not real, feeling your body doesn't belong to you, remembering seems real, can't tell memories from dreams, a familiar place looks strange, flow watching TV, fantasy or daydream feels real, can ignore pain, sit staring into space, talk to yourself, act like different people in different situations, can't tell if you did something or just thought about doing it, find things you wrote or drew but can't remember doing, hear voices in your head, things look far away or in a fog.

11. Smith and Glass (1977). See also Luborsky *et al.* (1975), who found "insignificant differences in proportions of patients who improved." Also, Strupp and Hadley (1979) found professional therapy no better than equivalent time spent with untrained college professors.

12. This study in the journal *Behavioral and Brain Sciences* includes 24 lengthy replies in the Open Peer Review section and a rebuttal from the author. It is recommended reading.

13. Salkovskis (1989, p. 51). For an excellent book on treating phobic disorders using cognitive-behavioral methods in context see Ross (1994). See also Scott (1989).

14. Ofshe and Waters (1994, p. 301).

15. Incest survey by Diana Russel published in the 1978 book *The Secret Trauma* (Pendergrast, 1995, p. 49).

16. Tavris (1993).

17. Michael Yapko is a clinical psychologist who wrote the 1994 book *Suggestions of Abuse* (Pendergrast, 1995, p. 488). Also, in 1993 Poole and Lindsay did a survey of 86 randomly selected Ph.D. therapists with a substantial female client base. They found that over half said that they were sometimes "fairly certain" after the first session that they were dealing with a repressed-memory case. Since there are something like 250,000 therapists in the country, each with many clients, it is not hard to see why we have a nationwide epidemic of families destroyed by "recovered memories" induced by therapist expectations (see Pendergrast, 1995, pp. 489–491). Some therapists routinely asked patients to imagine abuse as an aid in recovering memory. Such visualizations can actually create memories that will be easily confused with real memories (Loftus and Ketcham, 1994).

18. From a 1993 survey of the False Memory Syndrome Foundation (Neisser, 1994, p. 4).

19. Ofshe and Waters (1994, p. 178).

20. From the book *Ritual Abuse: What It Is, Why It Happens, How to Help* (Smith, 1993, p. 77).

21. Survey in Ofshe and Waters (1994, p. 178).

CHAPTER NINE: THE INFANT BRAIN

1. Winson (1985, p. 167).

2. Shatz (1992, p. 61).

3. Joseph (1993, p. 80).

4. Lieberman (1991, p. 18).

5. Barinaga (1995, p. 200).

6. PET, positron emission tomography. See Raichle (1994) for color photographs of brain activity during various tasks.

7. Gleik (1987, p. 8).

8. Smith and Sugar (1975); also Blakeslee (1980, p. 149).

9. This may be a hardware development requiring stimulation during a critical period similar to that for vision of vertical and horizontal lines.

10. Lieberman (1991, p. 147). Nine different studies referenced.

11. Merlin (1991, p. 12).

12. Since the right side has more free space. Experiments have demonstrated how the competition for space determines where abilities will develop. When nerves to certain fingers on a monkey were cut, experimenters found that the areas of the brain controlling finger movements rearranged themselves with more space dedicated to the still-functional fingers. This space came from areas that used to control the areas that were cut, indicating a kind of competition for brain space. See Edelman (1985).

13. Wingate (1976, p. 93); also Blakeslee (1980, p. 93).

14. Hecaen and De Ajuriagueira (1964, p. 77).

15. Jones (1966); also Blakeslee (1980, p. 93).

16. Berk (1989, p. 465).

17. Berk (1989, p. 466).

18. Gopnik (1993, p. 7).

19. Berk (1989, p. 542).

CHAPTER TEN: NONVERBAL THINKING

1. Austin (1974, p. 103).

2. Mehrabian (1972) cited in Masters and Johnson (1982, p. 250).

3. Barlow (1980, p. 81).

4. Gott (1973).

5. Russel (1983, p. 49).

6. Hadamard (1945, p. 84).

7. Mozart quote in Hadamard (1945, p. 16). See also Pearce (1974, p. 147).

8. Harris (1976, p. 196).

9. Money (1980, p. 127). Sonograms sometimes catch male fetuses in the womb with erections (Money, 1986, p. 16). Spinal cats (with their spinal cord severed) can walk and even change the way they walk without guidance from their brain. Male roaches continue copulation after decapitation by the female (Dretske, 1988, p. 4).

10. Solomon (1976, p. 247).

11. Merlin (1993, p. 739).

12. Searle (1992, p. 144), Solomon (1978, p. 163).

13. For Sufi see Baumeister (1991, p. 180). For Zen and Yoga see Baumeister (1991, pp. 192–193).

14. Csikszentmihalyi (1990). Baumeister (1991) develops the idea that suicide, drug addiction, and masochism are all attempts to silence the self.

CHAPTER ELEVEN: LOVE—MERGING THE SELF

1. For step-by-step drawings of this development see Figure 3-3 in Money (1980).

2. One survey asked men and women how many sexual partners they would ideally like to have over various time intervals. The men's preferences were three to four times higher than the women's (Buss and Schmitt, 1993, p. 211).

3. For a study of male/female preferences of 37 peoples in 33 countries, see Fisher (1992, p. 47).

4. Walsh (1991, p. 182).

5. Buss and Schmitt (1993, p. 204).

6. 84% allow polygamy (Fisher, 1992, pp. 66–69).

7. PEA addiction may be the basis of romance addiction. MAO inhibitors, which reduce PEA, help romance junkies (see Fisher, 1992, pp. 52–54). Dr. Thomas Insel and Dr. Sue Carter's research with prairie voles, a small mammal that bonds for life, has found that after mating males have a large increase in vasopressin in their brain. Mating causes a dramatic behavior change with strong bonding to one female. On female voles, the magic chemical seemed to be oxytocin, the same chemical used to trigger uterine contractions and milk production in women (*Nature*, 1994).

8. See Fisher (1992, p. 43).

9. See Money (1980, p. 74).

10. Money (1980, p. 122).

11. See Marshall (1983, p. 107). Another unconscious contributor to the process of falling in love is the fact that we tend to like a face more when we have seen it repeatedly. Experimenter Robert Zajonic proved this by showing subjects pictures of faces and then testing their preferences. The more they had seen a particular face, the more they liked it (Gazzaniga, 1988, p. 169).

12. Perls (1969) read verbatim to see just how much a skilled observer of nonverbal communications can see. He believes that repression is a fallacy and that only the words are blocked. "We have blocked one side, and then the self-expression comes out somewhere else, in our movements, in our posture, and most of all in our voice. A good therapist doesn't listen to the bullshit the patient produces, but to the sound, to the music, to the hesitations. Verbal communications is usually a lie. The real communications is beyond words."

13. Jankowiak and Fischer (1992).

14. Solomon (1988, pp. 48–49).

15. Fisher (1992, pp. 109–113).

16. For extramarital sex see Walsh (1991, p. 236). One study found that out of 34 male deaths during coitus, 27 of them occurred with mistresses (Gazzaniga, 1988, p. 176).

17. Some people have a working vomeronasal system. This separate smell system with separate direct connections to the reptilian brain is a vestige from our evolutionary past. See Rivlin and Gravelle (1984, pp. 149–153).

18. See Ackerman (1990, p. 9).

19. Quote from "The Fleece" in *Flowers of Evil*.

CHAPTER TWELVE:
THE EMPTY SELF

1. The suicide rate among teenagers has tripled in the past 30 years. Victims tend to be solitary boys who hold themselves to a high standard. Suicide is rare before the age of 12, which is when awareness of self becomes acute (Berk, 1989, box 11.1).

2. Population statistics and the concept of the empty self from Cushman (1990, p. 603).

3. Sampson (1988, p. 19).

4. Of course, some black, gay, and women's groups exist that have a positive attitude and can actually help people to be accepted into mainstream society; however, the victim approach seems to have more appeal in recent years. The double-positive-feedback of bad feelings it encourages are exactly the same as the attitudes that cause wars.

5. For a wonderfully done full-length discussion of the meaning of life and the importance and logic of emotions see Solomon (1976). Also read *The Magus* by John Fowles.

APPENDIX ONE:
THE COGNITIVE REVOLUTION

1. Note that the division is not between the right and left eye. Both eyes connect to both sides of the brain, but the light-sensitive retina in each eye is divided into a left and right half, each connected to one half of the brain.

2. Sperry (1968b, p. 726).

3. Sperry (1966).

4. Sperry (1968b, p. 318).

5. Gazzaniga (1985, p. 126). Dr. Gazzaniga's excellent book *The Social Brain* (Basic Books, 1985) is highly recommended if you want to learn more about these experiments. Though he earlier advanced his theory of the "verbal interpreter" in other writings, this one is the most readable presentation. My self module concept is a direct outgrowth of his ideas about a verbal interpreter module in the left hemisphere.

6. Gazzaniga (1985, p. 72).

7. To quote the doctor's report, "Following complete section of the corpus callosum no disturbance in visual, auditory, and tactile gnosis [sensation] was observed and praxis [movement] and language functions were unimpaired" (Akelaitis, 1944).

8. Women's brains may be less lateralized as a result of the earlier maturation of their brain structure. Boys spend more years with their brain hemispheres essentially isolated by incompletely developed connections between the hemispheres. This encourages more specialization (Blakeslee, 1980, pp. 102–108).

9. Witelson (1977).

10. Waber (1976). For a full-length book on sex differences in the brain see LeVay (1993). Dyslexia (reading disability) and stuttering, both problems of lateralization, are rare in girls but fairly common in boys.

11. Sperry wrote extensively defending the downward causation idea, which initially met much resistance when he first proposed it in 1965. See Sperry (1992, 1993).

Selected Bibliography

Ahern, Geoffrey, *et al.* (1993). The association of multiple personality and temporolimbic epilepsy. *Archives of Neurology, 50,* 1020–1025.

Ackerman, Diane. (1990). *A natural history of the senses.* New York: Random House.

Akelaitis, A. J. (1944). A study of gnosis, praxis, and language following section of the corpus callosum and anterior commissures. *Journal of Neurosurgery, 1,* 94–102.

Austin, G., Hayward, W., & Rouhe, S. (1974). A note on the problem of conscious man and cerebral disconnection by hemispherectomy. In M. Kinsbourne & A. Smith (Eds.), *Hemispheric disconnection and cerebral function.* Springfield, IL: Charles C. Thomas.

Baars, Bernard J. (1993). Why volition is a foundation problem for psychology. *Consciousness and Cognition, 2,* 281–309.

Barinaga, Marcia. (1995). Dendrites shed their dull image. *Science, 268,* 200–201.

Barlow, H. B. (1980). Nature's joke: A conjecture on the biological role of consciousness. In *Consciousness and the physical world* (pp. 81–93). B. D. Josephson, & Romachandran (Eds.), New York: Pergamon Press.

Barton, Charles. (1993). Backstage in psychiatry: The multiple personality controversy. *Dissociation, 6*(3), 167–172.

Barton, Scott. (1994). Chaos, self-organization, and psychology. *American Psychologist, 49*(1), 5–14.

Baumeister, Roy. (1987). How the self became a problem: A psychological review of historical research. *Journal of Personality and Social Psychology, 52*(1), 163–176.

Baumeister, Roy F. (1991). *Escaping the self.* New York: Basic Books.

Beahrs, John O. (1982). *Unity and multiplicity.* New York: Brunner/Mazel.

Beaton, Alan. (1985). *Left side right side: A review of laterality research.* New Haven: Yale University Press.

Berk, Laura A. (1989). *Child development.* Boston: Allyn & Bacon.

Bernstein, Eve, & Putnam, Frank W. (1986). Development, reliability, and validity of a dissociation scale. *Journal of Nervous and Mental Disease, 174*(12), 727–735.

Blakeslee, Thomas R. (1980). *The right brain.* New York: Doubleday.

Buss, David, & Schmitt, David. (1993). Sexual strategies theory: An evolutionary perspective on human mating. *Psychological Review, 100*(2), 204–232.

Butz, Michael. (1992). The fractal nature of the development of the self. *Psychological Reports, 71,* 1043–1063.

Calvin, William. (1991). *The throwing madonna.* New York: New Sciences.

Churchland, Patricia Smith. (1986). *Neurophilosophy.* Cambridge, MA: MIT Press.

Congdon, Tim. (1988). *The debt threat.* Oxford: Blackwell.

Crick, Francis. (1994). *The astonishing hypothesis.* New York: Scribner's.

Crick, Francis, & Koch, Christof. (1992, September). The problem of consciousness. *Scientific American*, pp.152–159.

Csikszentmihalyi, Mihaly. (1990). *Flow*. New York: Harper & Row.

Csikszentmihalyi, Mihaly. (1993). *The evolving self*. New York: Harper Collins.

Cushman, Phillip. (1990). Why the self is empty: Toward a historically situated psychology. *American Psychologist*, 45(5), 599–611. *Excellent ideas inspired part of Chapter Eleven.*

Cytowic, Richard. (1993). *The man who tasted shapes*. New York: Putnam. *An excellent book on doctors, synesthesia, and the mind.*

Davies, Paul. (1988). *The cosmic blueprint*. New York: Simon & Schuster.

Davis, Penelope J., & Schwartz. (1987). Repression and the inaccessibility of affective memories. *Journal of Personality and Social Psychology, 52*(1), 155–162.

Dawkins, Richard. (1976). *The selfish gene*. London: Oxford University Press.

Dawkins, Richard. (1986). *The blind watchmaker*. New York: Norton.

De Bono, Edward. (1990). *I am right you are wrong*. New York: Viking.

Dell, Paul F. (1988). Professional skepticism about multiple personality. *Journal of Nervous and Mental Disease, 176*(9), 528–537 (includes discussion).

Della Barba, Gianfranco. (1993). Confabulation: Knowledge and recollective experience. *Cognitive Neuropsychology, 10*(1), 1–20.

Dennett, Daniel. (1991). *Consciousness explained*. Boston: Little, Brown. *A very interesting but technical treatment of consciousness from the philosophical point of view. A source of many of the ideas in this book.*

Dennett, Daniel. (1992). Filling in versus finding out: A ubiquitous confusion in cognitive science. In H. L. Pick *et al.* (Eds.),

Cognition: Conceptual & methodological issues. Washington, DC: American Psychological Association.

Dennett, Daniel. Commentary by peers on Dennett's work fills the whole issue of *Consciousness and Cognition,* Volume 2, No. 1, Academic Press, March, 1993. *This journal is generally filled with discussions related to the subject of this book.*

Dennett, Daniel, & Kinsbourne, Marcel. (1992). Time and the observer: The where and when of consciousness in the brain. *Behavioral and Brain Sciences, 15,* 183–247. *An excellent debate on the timing of perception.*

Doi, Takeo. (1985). *The anatomy of self.* New York: Kodansha Intl.

Dretske, Fred I. (1988). *Explaining behavior: Reasons in a world of causes.* Cambridge, MA: MIT Press.

Edelman, Gerald. (1985). Neural Darwinism. In Michael Schafto (Ed.), *How we know.* New York: Harper & Row.

Edelman, Gerald. (1992). *Bright air brilliant fire.* New York: Basic Books. *Technical but good treatment by a Nobel prize-winner on the evolution of consciousness and neural Darwinism.*

Erdmann, Erica, & Stower, David. (1991). *Beyond a world divided: Human values in the brain–mind science of Roger Sperry.* Boston: Shambala.

Eysenck, Michael W. (1990). *The Blackwell dictionary of cognitive psychology.* Oxford: Blackwell.

Fast, Julius. (1970). *Body language.* New York: M. Evans.

Feldman-Summers, Shirly, & Pope, Kenneth S. (1994). The experience of "forgetting" childhood abuse: A national survey of psychologists. *Journal of Consulting and Clinical Psychology, 62*(3), 636–639.

Ferris, Timothy. (1992). *The mind's sky.* New York: Bantam.

Fisher, H. (1992). *The anatomy of love.* New York: Ingram.

Fisher, Seymour. (1954). The role of expectancy in the performance of posthypnotic behavior. *Journal of Abnormal and Social Psychology, 49,* 503.

Fromm, Erik, & Shor, Ronald. (Eds.). (1979). *Hypnosis: Developments in research and new perspectives.* New York: Aldine.

Excellent argument against the trance state paradigm, pages 217–265.

Gardner, Howard. (1985). *The mind's new science: The cognitive revolution.* New York: Basic Books.

Gardner, Martin. (1957). *Fads and fallacies in the name of science.* New York: Dover.

Gardner, Martin. (1992). *On the wild side.* New York: Prometheus.

Gazzaniga, Michael. (1985). *The social brain.* New York: Basic Books. *A very well-written book written by Sperry's assistant on the first split-brain experiments presenting evidence for modules and suggesting that a verbal interpreter in the left brain makes up stories to explain behavior driven by other modules. A source of many of the ideas in this book.*

Gazzaniga, Michael. (1978). *The integrated mind.* New York: Plenum Press.

Gazzaniga, Michael S. (1988). *Mind matters.* Boston: Houghton Mifflin.

Gazzaniga, Michael. (1992). *Nature's mind.* New York: Basic Books.

Gianotti, Guido, Caltagirone, & Zoccolotti. (1993). Left/right and cortical/subcortical dichotomies in the neuropsychological study of human emotions. *Cognition and Emotion, 7*(1), 71–93.

Gilovich, Thomas. (1991). *How we know what isn't so.* New York: Free Press.

Gleik, James. (1987). *Chaos.* New York: Viking. *A good introduction to mathematical chaos theory.*

Gold, Steven. (1994, May). Degrees of repression of sexual abuse memories. *American Psychologist.*

Goleman, Daniel. (1985). *Vital lies and simple truths.* New York: Simon & Schuster. *An excellent book on false beliefs and memory errors.*

Gopnik, Alison. (1993). How we know our minds: The illusion of first-person knowledge of intentionality. *Behavioral and*

Brain Sciences, 16, 1–14. *A key article on how children learn the concept of intentions.*

Gott, Peggy S. (1973). Cognitive abilities following right and left hemispherectomy. *Cortex, 9,* 266–273.

Greenwald, Anthony. (1992, June). Unconscious cognition reclaimed. *American Psychologist,* pp. 766–777.

Guidano, Vittorio F. (1987). *Complexity of the self: A developmental approach to psychopathology and therapy.* New York: Guilford Press.

Hadamard, Jacques. (1945). *The psychology of invention in the mathematical field.* New York: Dover Publications.

Hadley, & Strupp, Hans H. (1976). Contemporary views on negative effects in psychotherapy. *Psychiatry, 33,* 1291–1294.

Hamachek, Don. (1971). *Encounters with the self.* New York: Holt, Rinehart.

Harris, Harold. (Ed.). (1976). *Astride the two cultures.* New York: Random House.

Harth, Erich. (1992). *Windows on the mind.* New York: Morrow.

Hecaen, H., & De Ajuriagueira, J. (1964). *Left handedness: Manual superiority and cerebral dominance* (E. Ponder, transl.). New York: Grune & Stratton.

Heelas, Paul, & Lock, Andrew. (Eds.). (1981). *Indigenous psychologies: The anthropology of the self.* New York: Academic Press.

Hilgard, Ernst R. (1977). *Divided consciousness.* New York: Wiley.

Humphry, Nicholas. (1992). *A history of the mind.* New York: Simon & Schuster.

Hunt, Morton. (1982). *The universe within.* New York: Simon & Schuster.

Ischlondsky, N. Dorin. (1955). The inhibitory process in the cerebrophysical laboratory and in the clinic. *Journal of Nervous and Mental Disease, 121,* 5–18.

James, William. (1980). *Principles of psychology,* Vol 1. Fawcet (1963, p. 294).

Jankowiak, W. R., & Fischer, E. F. (1992). A cross-cultural perspective on romantic love. *Ethnology, 31*(2), 149–155.

Jaynes, Julian. (1976). *The origin of consciousness in the breakdown of the bicameral mind.* Boston: Houghton Mifflin.

Jennings, Jesse, & Hoebel, D. (Eds.) (1955). *Readings in anthropology.* New York: McGraw-Hill.

Jones, R. K. (1966). Observations on stammering after localized cerebral injury. *Journal of Neurology, Neurosurgery, and Psychiatry, 29,* 192–195.

Josepf, R. (1986). Confabulation and delusional denial: Frontal lobe and lateralized influences. *Journal of Clinical Psychology, 42*(3), 507–519.

Joseph, R. (1993). *The naked neuron.* New York: Plenum Press.

Kahn, Lloyd. (1973). *Shelter.* Bolinas, CA: Shelter Publications.

Karmiloff-Smith, Annette. (1994). Precis of beyond modularity: A developmental perspective on cognitive science. *Behavioral and Brain Sciences, 17,* 693–745.

Kauffman, Stuart A. (1991, August). Antichaos and adaptation. *Scientific American,* pp. 78–84.

Kluft, Richard P. (1993). The initial stages of psychotherapy in the treatment of multiple personality disorder patients. *Dissociation, 6*(2), 145–160.

Koestler, Arthur. (1967). *The ghost in the machine.* New York: Macmillan Co. *An excellent book on self organization.*

Kosslyn, Stephen M., & Koenig, Oliver. (1992). *Wet mind: The new cognitive neuroscience.* New York: Macmillan Co. *An interesting but technical book with a computer approach to consciousness.*

LeVay, Simon. (1993). *The sexual brain.* Cambridge, MA: MIT Press.

Lewin, Roger. (1992). *Complexity.* New York: Macmillan Co.

Lieberman, Philip. (1991). *Uniquely human.* Cambridge, MA: Harvard.

Liebowitz, Michael R. (1983). *The chemistry of love.* Boston: Little, Brown.

Linville, Patricia. (1987). Self-complexity as a cognitive buffer against stress-related illness and depression. *Journal of Personality and Social Psychology, 52*(4), 663–676.

Loftus, Elizabeth, & Ketcham, Katherine. (1991). *Witness for the defense*. New York: St. Martin's Press.

Loftus, Elizabeth, & Ketcham, Katherine. (1994). *The myth of repressed memory*. New York: St. Martin's Press.

London, Perry, & Klerman, Gerald L. (1982). Evaluating psychotherapy. *American Journal of Psychiatry, 139*(6), 709–717.

Luborsky, Lester, Singer, Barton, & Luborsky, Lise. (1975). Comparative studies of psychotherapies: Is it true that "everyone has won and all must have prizes?" *Archives of General Psychiatry, 32*, 995–1008.

Lyons, Arthur. (1988). *Satan wants you*. New York: Mysterious Press.

Lyons, John D. (1978). *The invention of self*. Carbondale: University of Southern Illinois Press.

McCrone, John. (1991). *The ape that spoke*. New York: Morrow.

McHugh, Paul R. (1992). Psychiatric misadventures. *American Scholar, 61*(4), 497–510.

McKellar, Peter. (1979). *Mindsplit*. London: J. M. Dent.

Margulis, Lynn, & Sagan, Dorian. (1986). *Microcosmos: Four billion years of microbial evolution*. New York: Summit Books. *A wonderful book about self-organization and nature at the cell level. Read it!*

Marshall, Evan. (1983). *Eye language*. New York: New Trend.

Masters & Johnson. (1982). *Sex and human loving*. Boston: Little, Brown.

Merlin, Donald. (1991). *Origins of the modern mind*. Cambridge, MA: Harvard University Press.

Merlin, Donald. (1993). Precis of origins of the modern mind: Three stages of evolution of culture and cognition. *Behavioral and Brain Sciences, 16*, 737–791.

Merskey, Harold. (1994). The artifactual nature of multiple personality disorder. *Dissociation, 6*(3), 173–177 (includes rejoinder by Charles Barton).

Meyers, David. (1992). *The pursuit of happiness*. New York: Morrow.

Meyers, Gerald E. (1969). *Self: An introduction to philosophical psychology*. New York: Pegasus.

Moir, Anne, & Jessel, David. (1989). *Brain sex*. New York: Dell.

Money, John. (1980). *Love and love sickness*. Baltimore: Johns Hopkins Press.

Money, John. (1986). *Love maps*. New York: Irvington.

Murphy, Patricia Engle. (1994). Dissociative experiences and dissociative disorders in a non-clinical university student group. *Dissociation, 6*(1), 28–35.

Neisser, Ulric. (1994). Self narratives: True and false. In Ulrick Neisser & Robyn Fivush (Eds.), *The remembering self*. London: Cambridge University Press.

Neisser, Ulric, & Harsch, Nicole. (1992). Phantom flashbulbs: False recollections of hearing the news about Challenger. In Eugene Winograd *et al*. (Eds.), *Affect and accuracy in recall*. London: Cambridge University Press.

Nesbit, Richard, & Wilson, Timothy. (1977). Telling more than we can know: Verbal reports on mental processes. *Psychological Review, 84*(3), 231–265.

Ofshe, Richard, & Waters, Ethan. (1994). *Making monsters*. New York: Scribner's.

Ornstein, Robert. (1972). *The psychology of consciousness*. San Francisco: Freeman.

Ornstein, Robert. (1991). *The evolution of consciousness*. New York: Touchstone. *An easy-reading presentation of the modular concept of the mind. Calling nonverbal modules "simpletons" is a mistake, however, as some of them are actually the very basis of creativity.*

Ortony, A., Clore, G., & Collins, A. (1988). *The cognitive structure of emotions*. London: Cambridge University Press.

Pearce, Joseph Clinton. (1974). *Exploring the crack in the cosmic egg*. New York: Julian Press.

Pendergrast, Mark. (1995). Victims of memory: *Incest accusations and shattered lives*. Hinesburg, VT: Upper Access Inc.

Penrose, Roger. (1989). *The emperor's new mind.* London: Oxford University Press.

Perls, Fredric. (1969). *Gestalt therapy verbatim.* Moab, VT: Real People Press.

Phelps, Michael, & Mazziotta, John. (1985). Positron emission tomography: Human brain function and biochemistry. *Science, 228*(4701), 799–809.

Prigatano, George, & Schacter, Davis. (1991). *Awareness of deficit after brain injury.* London: Oxford University Press.

Prigogine, Ilya, & Stenses, Isabelle. (1984). *Order out of chaos.* New York: Bantam Books.

Prioleau, Leslie, Murdock, Martha, & Brody, Nathan. (1983). An analysis of psychotherapy versus placebo studies. *Behavioral and Brain Sciences, 6,* 275–310. *Recommended. Includes peer review discussion.*

Radner, Dasie, & Radner, Michael. (1989). *Animal consciousness.* New York: Prometheus.

Raichle, Marcus E. (1994). Visualizing the mind. *Scientific American, 270*(4), 58–65. *PET scans in color.*

Rakic, Pasco, *et al.* (1966). Concurrent overproduction of synapses in diverse regions of the primate cerebral cortex. *Science, 232,* 232–234.

Restak, Richard. (1991). *The brain has a mind of its own.* New York: Harmony.

Restak, Richard M. (1994). *The modular brain.* New York: Scribner's.

Rivlin, Robert, & Gravelle, Karen. (1984). *Deciphering the senses.* New York: Simon & Schuster.

Rosenfield, Israel. (1988). *The invention of memory.* New York: Basic Books.

Rosenfield, Israel. (1992). *The strange, familiar, and forgotten.* New York: Knopf.

Rosenweig, Saul. (1988). The identity and idiodynamics of the multiple personality "Sally Beauchamp." *American Psychologist, 43*(1), 45–48.

Ross, Colin. (1991). The dissociated self and the cultural dissociation barrier. *Dissociation, 4*(1), 55–61.

Ross, Jerilyn. (1994). *Triumph over fear.* New York: Bantam Books.
*An excellent book on contextual cognitive-behavioral therapy for
phobias.*

Rowan, John. (1990). *Subpersonalities: The people inside us.* London: Routledge.

Sacks, Oliver. (1970). *The man who mistook his wife for a hat.* New
York: Harper. *A very entertaining account of several right hemisphere damage cases.*

Salkovskis, Paul M. (1989). Obsessions and compulsions. In Jan
Scott, Mark Williams, & Aaron Beck (Eds.), *Cognitive therapy
and clinical practice.* London: Routledge.

Sampson, Edward E. (1985). The decentralization of identity.
American Psychologist, 49(11), 1203–1211.

Sampson, Edward. (1988). The debate on individualism: Indigenous psychologies of the individual and their role in personal and societal functioning. *American Psychologist, 43*(1),
15–22.

Sanders, Barbara. (1992). The imaginary companion in multiple
personality disorder. *Dissociation, 5*(3), 159–162.

Schacter, Daniel. (1992). Understanding implicit memory: A cognitive neuroscience approach. *American Psychologist, 47*(4),
559–569.

Schieve, William C., & Allyn, Peter M. (Eds.). (1982). *Self-organization and dissipative structures: Applications in the physical
and social sciences.* Austin: University of Texas.

Schnabel, Jim. (1994). Chronic claims of alien abduction and
some other traumas as self victimization syndromes. *Dissociation, 6*(1), 51–59.

Scott, Jan, Williams, J. Mark, & Beck, Aaron. (Eds.). (1989).
Cognitive therapy in clinical practice. New York: Routledge.

Searle, John R. (1992). *The rediscovery of the mind.* Cambridge,
MA: MIT Press.

Shatz, Carla. (1992, September). The developing brain. *Scientific American*, p. 61.

Smith, Aaron, & Sugar, Oscar. (1975). Development of above normal language and intelligence 21 years after left hemispherectomy. *Neurology, 25*, 813–818.

Smith, Elliot, & Miller, Fredrick. (1978). Limits on perception of cognitive processes: A reply to Nesbit and Wilson. *Psychological Review, 85*(4), 355–362.

Smith, Margaret. (1993). *Ritual abuse: What it is, why it happens, how to help.* New York: Harper Collins.

Smith, Mary Lee, & Glass, Gene V. (1977). Meta-analysis of psychotherapy outcome studies. *American Psychologist*, pp. 752–760.

Solomon, Robert C. (1976). *The passions.* New York: Doubleday. *An excellent book on the logic of emotions and the meaning in life. A source of many of the ideas in Chapters Ten and Eleven.*

Solomon, Robert C. (1988). *About love.* New York: Simon & Schuster.

Spanos, Nicholas P. (1986). Hypnotic behavior: A social-psychological interpretation of amnesia, analgesis, and "trance logic." *Behavioral and Brain Sciences, 9*, 449–502. *An excellent discussion with many peer comments and a rebuttal.*

Spanos, Nicholas P., Radtke, H. Lorraine, & Bertrand, Lorne D. (1985). Hypnotic amnesia as a strategic enactment: Breaching amnesia in highly susceptible subjects. *Journal of Personality and Social Psychology, 47*(5), 1155–1169.

Spanos, Nicholas P., *et al.* (1991). Secondary identity enactments during hypnotic past-life regression: A sociocognitive perspective. *Journal of Personality and Social Psychology, 61*(2), 308–320.

Sperry, R. W. (1966). Brain bisection and mechanisms of consciousness. In John C. Eccles (Ed.), *Brain and conscious experience.* Berlin: Springer-Verlag.

Sperry, R. W. (1968a). Mental unity following disconnection of the cerebral hemispheres. *Harvey Lectures, Series 62.* New York: Academic Press.

Sperry, R. W. (1968b). Hemisphere disconnection and conscious awareness. *American Psychologist, 23*, 723–733.

Sperry, Roger. (1982). Some effects of disconnecting the cerebral hemispheres. *Science, 217*, 1223–1226.

Sperry, R. W. (1991). A defense of mentalism and emergent interaction. *The Journal of Mind and Behavior, 12*(2), 221–246.

Sperry, R. W. (1992). Turnabout on consciousness: A mentalist view. *The Journal of Mind and Behavior, 13*(3), 259–280.

Sperry, Roger. (1993). The impact and promise of the cognitive revolution. *American Psychologist, 48*(8), 878–885.

Steinberg, Robert J., & Barnes, Michael L. (Eds.). (1988). *The psychology of love*. New Haven: Yale University Press.

Strupp, H. H., & Hadley, Suzanne. (1979). Specific vs nonspecific factors in psychotherapy. *Archives of General Psychiatry, 36*, 1125–1136.

Szasz, Thomas. (1970). *The manufacture of madness*. New York: Harper & Row.

Tart, Charles T. (1975). *Discrete states of consciousness*. New York: Dutton.

Tavris, Carol. (1993, January 3). Beware the incest survivor machine. *New York Times Book Review*, p. 1.

Taylor, Charles. (1989). *Sources of the self*. Cambridge, MA: Harvard University Press.

Terr, Lenore. (1994). *Unchained memories*. New York: Basic Books.

Velmans, Max. (1991). Is human information processing conscious? *Behavioral and Brain Sciences, 14*, 651–726; also commentary in *Behavioral and Brain Sciences*, 1993, *16*(2), 404–415.

Waber, Deborah P. (1976). Sex differences in cognition: A function of maturation rate? *Science, 192*, 572–573.

Waldrop, Mitchell. (1992). *Complexity*. New York: Simon & Schuster.

Walsh, Anthony. (1991). *The science of love*. Buffalo, NY: Prometheus Books.

Warwick, Hilary, & Salkovskis, Paul. (1989). Hypochondriasis. In Jan Scott, Mark Williams, & Aaron Beck (Eds.), *Cognitive therapy and clinical practice*. London: Routledge.

Watts, Allen. (1977). *The essence of Alan Watts*. Millbrae, CA: Celestial Arts.

Weinstein, Edwin A., & Lyerly. (1968). Confabulation following brain injury. *Archives of General Psychiatry, 18,* 348–353.

Wessler, Richard, & Hankin-Wessler. (1989). Nonconscious algorithms in cognitive and affective process. *Journal of Cognitive Psychotherapy, 3*(4), 243–253.

Wingate, Marcel E. (1976). *Stuttering: Theory and treatment*. New York: Irvington.

Winson, Jonathan. (1985). *Brain and psyche*. New York: Doubleday.

Witelson, Sandra F. (1977). Early hemisphere specialization and interhemispheric plasticity. In S. Segalowitz & F. Gruber (Eds.), *Language development and neurological plasticity*. New York: Academic Press.

Wood, Garth. (1983). *The myth of neurosis*. New York: Harper & Row.

Wright, Robert. (19940. *The moral animal. The new science of evolutionary psychology*. New York: Pantheon.

Wynn, Ralph. (1956). *Hypnotism made easy*. North Hollywood: Wilshire Book.

Zeki, Semir. (1992, September). The visual image in mind and brain. *Scientific American,* pp. 69–74.

Index

DATE			